★ It's My State! ★ ★ ★ ★ ★

OHIO

The Buckeye State

Joyce Hart, Lisa M. Herrington, and Kerry Jones Waring

Cavendish Square

New York

Published in 2017 by Cavendish Square Publishing, LLC
243 5th Avenue, Suite 136, New York, NY 10016

Third Edition

Website: cavendishsq.com

This publication represents the opinions and views of the author based on his or her personal experience, knowledge, and research. The information in this book serves as a general guide only. The author and publisher have used their best efforts in preparing this book and disclaim liability rising directly or indirectly from the use and application of this book.

CPSIA Compliance Information: Batch #CS16CSQ

All websites were available and accurate when this book was sent to press.

Library of Congress Cataloging-in-Publication Data
Names: Hart, Joyce, 1954- author. | Herrington, Lisa M., author. | Waring, Kerry Jones, author.
Title: Ohio / Joyce Hart, Lisa M. Herrington, and Kerry Jones Waring.
Description: New York : Cavendish Square Publishing, [2016] | Series: It's my state! | Includes index. | Description based on print version record and CIP data provided by publisher; resource not viewed.
Identifiers: LCCN 2016001505 (print) | LCCN 2016001280 (ebook) | ISBN 9781627131711 (ebook) | ISBN 9781627131698 (library bound)
Subjects: LCSH: Ohio--Juvenile literature.
Classification: LCC F491.3 (print) | LCC F491.3 .H37 2016 (ebook) | DDC 977.1--dc23
LC record available at http://lccn.loc.gov/2016001505

Editorial Director: David McNamara
Editor: Fletcher Doyle
Copy Editor: Nathan Heidelberger
Art Director: Jeffrey Talbot
Designer: Alan Sliwinski
Production Assistant: Karol Szymczuk
Photo Research: J8 Media

Printed in the United States of America

OHIO

CONTENTS

State Tree: Ohio Buckeye

Ohio is nicknamed the Buckeye State because of its many buckeye trees. The buckeye tree got its name from the Iroquois, who noticed that the nutlike seeds of the fruit looked like the eyes of a buck (a male deer). The sports teams at Ohio State are known as the Buckeyes.

State Bird: Cardinal

Cardinals, once rare in Ohio, live throughout the state today. The cardinal was adopted as the state bird in 1933. The feathers of the male are usually red, while the female's feathers tend to be brown. A cardinal also has a distinctive tuft of feathers on the top of its head.

State Mammal: White-Tailed Deer

Although white-tailed deer are common throughout Ohio, most roam in the southeastern woodlands. They are the state's largest game animals. In 1988, the white-tailed deer was designated the state mammal. They have a horizontally split pupil that helps them see well at night.

OHIO ★ ★ ★ ★ ★

★ State Insect: Ladybug

In 1975, the ladybug, officially known as the ladybird beetle, was named Ohio's state insect. At the time, legislators compared the ladybug's qualities to the people of Ohio. They called the ladybug "proud and friendly" and "extremely industrious." Gardeners appreciate ladybugs because they feed on insects that can harm crops.

★ State Reptile: Black Racer

The black racer snake, named the state reptile in 1995, can be found throughout Ohio. Because the black racer eats disease-carrying rodents that damage crops, it is known as the "farmer's friend." Some of these speedy hunters have been recorded going 10 miles per hour (16 kilometers per hour).

★ State Fruit: Tomato

Tomatoes are an important crop in Ohio, a leading producer of tomato products. Elementary school students worked to help pass the bill that made the tomato Ohio's official state fruit in 2009. Several kinds of tomato are grown in Ohio, including heirloom, plum, cherry, and yellow varieties.

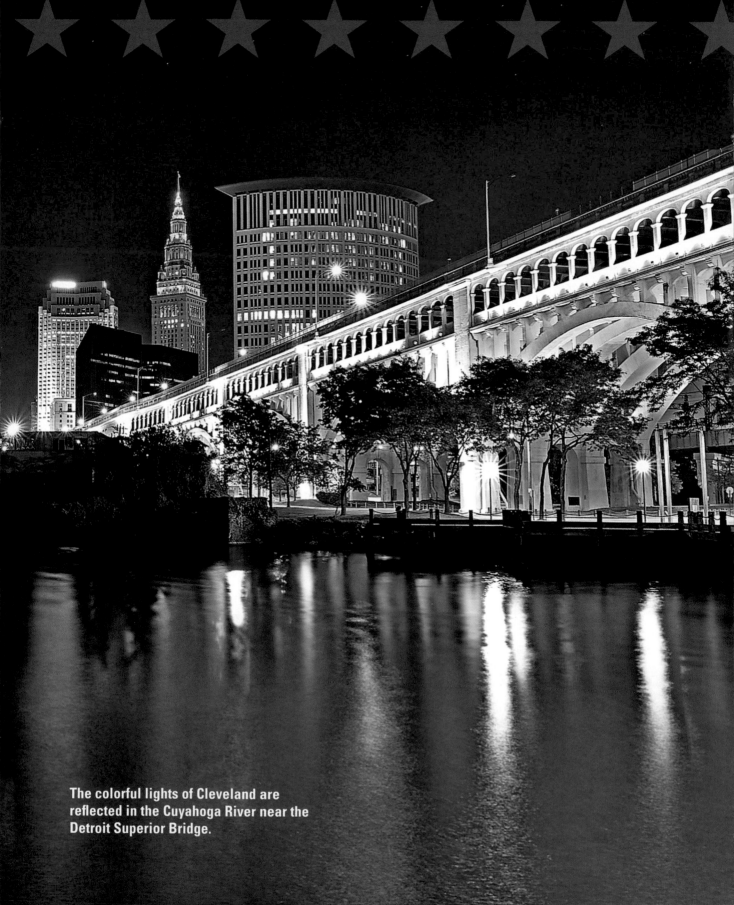

The colorful lights of Cleveland are reflected in the Cuyahoga River near the Detroit Superior Bridge.

The Buckeye State

1

L ocated in the Midwest, Ohio is known as the Buckeye State. It gets its nickname from the many buckeye trees native to the region. Ohio is a medium-size state. With a land area of 40,861 square miles (105,830 square kilometers), Ohio ranks thirty-fifth among the states. Ohio is divided into eighty-eight counties.

From rolling hills to flat plains and sandy beachfronts, Ohio is a combination of landscapes. The eastern border of the state starts as rolling plateaus (raised land) and slowly settles into flat plains toward the west. The state's northern border is largely made up of a long beachfront along Lake Erie. The majestic Ohio River cuts a curving trail from east to west across Ohio's southern border.

How Ohio Was Formed

Massive sheets of ice called glaciers moved slowly across much of Ohio about fifteen thousand years ago, during the last Ice Age. The glacial movement

Ohio Borders	
North:	Lake Erie
	Michigan
South:	Kentucky
	West Virginia
East:	Pennsylvania
	West Virginia
West:	Indiana

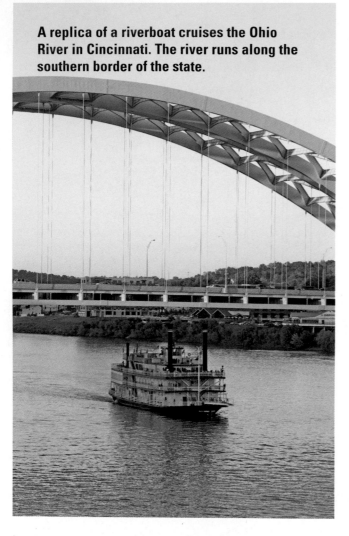

A replica of a riverboat cruises the Ohio River in Cincinnati. The river runs along the southern border of the state.

changed the landscape in many ways, flattening hills, filling valleys, and carving out the state's four primary land regions. Those regions are the Appalachian Plateau, the Bluegrass Region, the Till Plains, and the Lake Plains. As the glaciers melted, Lake Erie formed and then overflowed. The excess water eventually created a small stream, which grew in size over time and is today the Ohio River.

Underground streams in Ohio helped create caverns, or caves. In 1872, two boys, Peter Rutan and Henry Homer, discovered Seneca Caverns in Bellevue. Today, the caverns are a popular attraction for visitors to the area. Ohio Caverns, in West Liberty, were discovered in 1897. They are the largest caverns in Ohio, with more than 2 miles (3.2 kilometers) of known passageways.

The Appalachian Plateau

Most of the eastern half of Ohio is made up of the Appalachian Plateau. The northern part of this area contains rolling hills and valleys. The southern part of this area contains some of the steepest hills and deepest valleys in the most rugged part of the state. It is not a farming area because the soil is not very fertile. Although forests once covered most of the state, many of them have been cut down. However, some of the largest remaining forests, such as Wayne National Forest, still exist on the Appalachian Plateau.

Much of Ohio's richest mineral deposits are located on the Appalachian Plateau. Coal, for instance, was first found in Jefferson County, on Ohio's eastern border. Since that discovery, Ohio has become one of the country's biggest coal producing states. Natural gas and oil are also found there.

The city of Marietta is on the southern part of the Appalachian Plateau. East Liverpool, famous for its pottery, is also situated on the Appalachian Plateau. Athens,

Sumac adds vibrant color in the fall to the Wayne National Forest, which is located on the Appalachian Plateau.

Hocking, and Perry are some of the area's main coal-producing counties. Akron sits at the northern edge of the plateau. Its population is about two hundred thousand, making it Ohio's fifth-largest city.

The Bluegrass Region

When someone hears the term "Bluegrass Region," Kentucky usually comes to mind. But this region spills north from Kentucky into Ohio, too. Also referred to as the Lexington Plain, the Bluegrass Region, located in the southern part of the state, is the smallest land area in Ohio. It contains rolling hills that are covered in a thin layer of fertile soil. Adams Lake, a beautiful recreation area, and the Shawnee State Forest, one of the state's largest forests, are found here.

The Till Plains

The Till Plains, south of the Lake Plains, make up most of western Ohio. Although the region typically has low, rolling hills, both the highest and the lowest points in Ohio are located here. Campbell Hill, in Logan County, rises 1,550 feet (472 meters) above sea level. It is the state's highest point. At the southwestern corner of the state, along the Ohio River near Cincinnati, is Ohio's lowest point, measuring only 455 feet (139 m) above sea level. The hills of these plains are made up of soil and rocks that retreating glaciers left there as they melted at the end of the last Ice Age. Most of this area was completely covered in woodlands before white settlers moved into the region and discovered the rich soil.

OHIO

County	Population	County	Population	County	Population
Adams County	28,550	Hancock County	74,782	Paulding County	19,614
Allen County	106,331	Hardin County	32,058	Perry County	36,058
Ashland County	53,139	Harrison County	15,864	Pickaway County	55,698
Ashtabula County	101,497	Henry County	28,215	Pike County	28,709
Athens County	64,757	Highland County	43,589	Portage County	161,419
Auglaize County	45,949	Hocking County	29,380	Preble County	42,270
Belmont County	70,400	Holmes County	42,366	Putnam County	34,499
Brown County	44,846	Huron County	59,626	Richland County	124,475
Butler County	368,130	Jackson County	33,225	Ross County	78,064
Carroll County	28,836	Jefferson County	69,709	Sandusky County	60,944
Champaign County	40,097	Knox County	60,921	Scioto County	79,499
Clark County	138,333	Lake County	230,041	Seneca County	56,745
Clermont County	197,363	Lawrence County	62,450	Shelby County	49,423
Clinton County	42,040	Licking County	166,492	Stark County	375,586
Columbiana County	107,841	Logan County	45,858	Summit County	541,781
Coshocton County	36,901	Lorain County	301,356	Trumbull County	210,312
Crawford County	43,784	Lucas County	441,815	Tuscarawas County	92,582
Cuyahoga County	1,280,122	Madison County	43,435	Union County	52,300
Darke County	52,959	Mahoning County	238,823	Van Wert County	28,744
Defiance County	39,037	Marion County	66,501	Vinton County	13,435
Delaware County	174,214	Medina County	172,332	Warren County	212,693
Erie County	77,079	Meigs County	23,770	Washington County	61,778
Fairfield County	146,156	Mercer County	40,814	Wayne County	114,520
Fayette County	29,030	Miami County	102,506	Williams County	37,642
Franklin County	1,163,414	Monroe County	14,642	Wood County	125,488
Fulton County	42,698	Montgomery County	535,153	Wyandot County	22,615
Gallia County	30,934	Morgan County	15,054		
Geauga County	93,389	Morrow County	34,827		
Greene County	161,573	Muskingum County	86,074		
Guernsey County	40,087	Noble County	14,645		
Hamilton County	802,374	Ottawa County	41,428		

Source: US Bureau of the Census, 2010

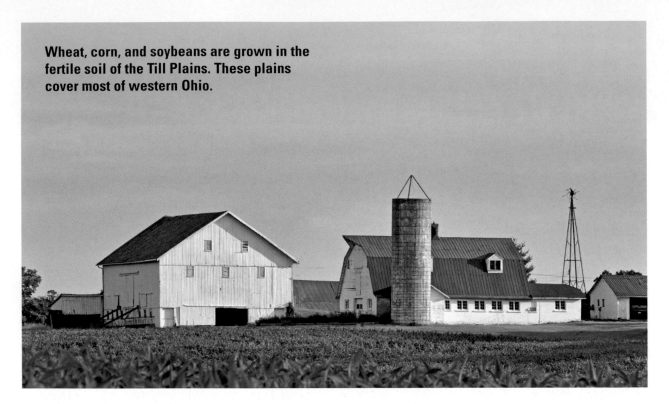

Wheat, corn, and soybeans are grown in the fertile soil of the Till Plains. These plains cover most of western Ohio.

The Till Plains have the most fertile soil in Ohio. The region is where most of the state's farms are located. Farmers here grow wheat, corn, and soybeans. They also raise cattle. The Corn Belt—an area where most of the corn in the United States is grown—begins in the Till Plains and extends west for many hundreds of miles.

The rich soil may have attracted many of the early white settlers, but in modern times, it is the large cities that draw new people. Cincinnati, Ohio's third-largest city with a population of about 297,000, lies to the south on the Till Plains. Dayton, the sixth-largest city, with about 141,000 people, is just a short drive north of Cincinnati. Columbus, the state's largest city and capital, is located in the center of the Till Plains. About 787,000 people live in Columbus.

The Lake Plains

The Lake Plains cover the entire northern portion of Ohio. Many different kinds of fruits and vegetables grow on the region's fertile land. Most of the Lake Plains follows the shoreline of Lake Erie. In the northeastern corner of the state, the plains extend only 5 to 10 miles (8 to 16 km) south of the lake. In the northwestern corner, however, they broaden to more than 50 miles (80 km).

With a population of about 397,000, Cleveland, Ohio's second-largest city, dominates this area. Located on Lake Erie, Cleveland is a busy manufacturing and shipping center. Other cities in this region, such as Toledo, Ohio's fourth-largest city (with more than

287,000 people), and Lorain, also have ports on Lake Erie. These ports allow them to ship their products to other states and countries.

The Waterways

Thousands of years ago, Ohio was covered with water. Today, much of that water has drained into tens of thousands of lakes and ponds, as well as 44,000 miles (70,800 km) of rivers and streams. The name "Ohio" comes from the Iroquois word *O-hy-o*, meaning "great river." The Iroquois first used the word to describe the river, and it later became the state's name.

Historic Flood

The greatest natural disaster in Ohio history happened in 1913, during an event called the Great Dayton Flood. The Miami River overflowed after a series of winter storms, and some parts of Dayton saw 20 feet [6 m] of flooding.

All the rivers and streams in the northern quarter of the state empty into Lake Erie. The other rivers drain into the Ohio River to the south. The major rivers in the state include the Ohio, Scioto, Miami, Sandusky, Huron, and Cuyahoga.

Lake Erie is Ohio's largest lake (although parts of the lake are in other states or in Canada). Erie is the second-smallest Great Lake, after Lake Ontario, but Lake Erie is not that small. It is

The Ohio River provided business opportunities that allowed Cincinnati to grow into an important city.

★ 10 ★ KEY SITES ★ ★ ★

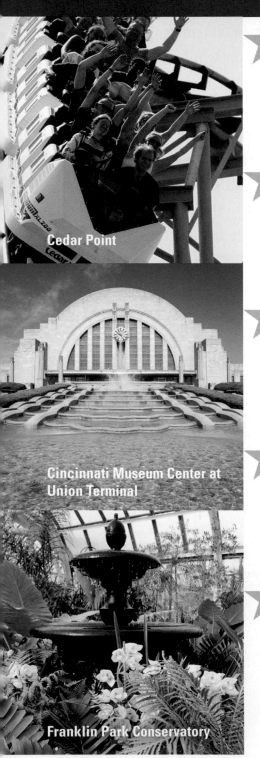

Cedar Point

Cincinnati Museum Center at Union Terminal

Franklin Park Conservatory

1. African Safari Wildlife Park

Visitors to this 100-acre (40.5-hectare) park in Port Clinton can drive through an authentic wild animal habitat, observing and feeding animals such as giraffes, buffaloes, and camels. There is a walkable area called Safari Junction.

2. Boonshoft Museum of Discovery

The Boonshoft Museum of Discovery is a children's museum and zoo in Dayton that features an extensive collection of both natural history artifacts and live animals. The museum is also home to a planetarium and observatory.

3. Cedar Point

Cedar Point is called "the Roller Coaster Capital of the World" and is the second-oldest operating amusement park in the United States. Visitors can enjoy the park's seventy-two rides, sixteen roller coasters, a beach, and an indoor water park.

4. Cincinnati Museum Center at Union Terminal

This unique-looking building operated as a railroad terminal for decades and has been used for many other purposes. Today it is home to museums, a library, and a theater, and is used as a rail station again.

5. Franklin Park Conservatory

Columbus's Franklin Park Conservatory was founded in 1852 as a site for the Franklin County Fair. Today, it is a leading site for **horticulture**—the study of plants—in Ohio and also a favorite location for weddings and other events.

6. Hocking Hills State Park

Located in the southern portion of the state, Hocking Hills State Park is home to many notable rock formations, waterfalls, and gorges. With more than two hundred campsites, the park attracts Ohioans who enjoy the outdoors.

7. National Underground Railroad Freedom Center

This Cincinnati museum is devoted to the Underground Railroad, the trail taken by escaping slaves up through the Civil War. The center's larger mission is to educate and to support freedom for enslaved people around the world.

8. Rock and Roll Hall of Fame

People from around the world come to the shores of Lake Erie in Cleveland to visit the Rock and Roll Hall of Fame. Every year, the museum **inducts**, or adds, bands or solo musicians that have had a major impact on music.

9. Steamship William G. Mather Maritime Museum

This freighter ship used to transport materials such as ore and coal throughout the Great Lakes, earning it the nickname "the ship that built Cleveland." In 1990, the ship was reopened as a museum on Cleveland's North Coast Harbor.

10. Toledo Museum of Art

More than thirty thousand works are on display at the Toledo Museum of Art. The museum covers 4 acres (1.6 ha) and contains forty-five galleries, fifteen classroom studios, and a theater.

Hocking Hills State Park

National Underground Railroad Freedom Center

Rock and Roll Hall of Fame

the twelfth-largest freshwater lake in the world, and it extends more than 200 miles (320 km) from east to west and about 57 miles (92 km) from north to south. Thousands of years ago, Lake Erie was much deeper. **Beach ridges**—sandy deposits that rise above the otherwise flat ground—are noticeable in some spots along the coastal plain in northwestern Ohio. These ridges mark the ancient shoreline and show how high the lake waters used to be. Today, Lake Erie's deepest point measures only about 200 feet (60 m). Several small islands in Lake Erie—Kelleys Island and the three Bass Islands—are part of Ohio and serve as popular recreation areas.

Ohioans enjoy other lakes, too. Some of the major lakes in Ohio are Berlin Lake, Seneca Lake, C. J. Brown Reservoir, and Grand Lake St. Marys (the largest lake entirely within Ohio).

The Climate

Ohio's climate is generally about the same for all regions of the state. This is partly due to the fact that the state has no very tall mountain ranges that can create different climate zones—either because of large differences in altitude or because the mountains block moving weather systems. When a weather system blows down from Canada or up from

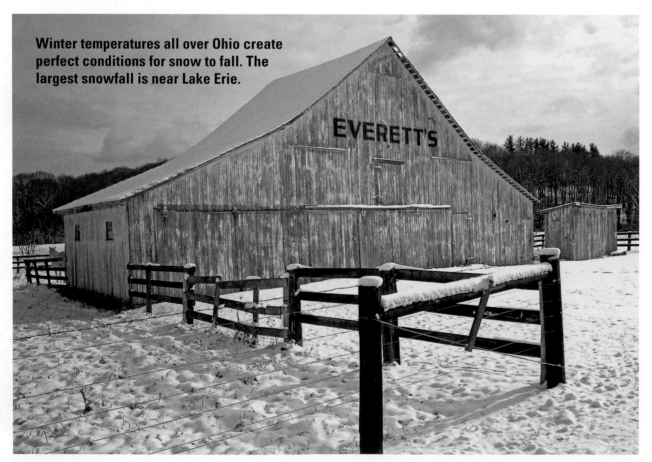

Winter temperatures all over Ohio create perfect conditions for snow to fall. The largest snowfall is near Lake Erie.

EVERETT'S

the Gulf of Mexico, nothing stops it from completely crossing Ohio. Sometimes, strong weather systems bring Ohioans very cold, very hot, or very stormy weather. Another factor affecting the state's climate is Lake Erie, which can make northern Ohio a bit colder in the spring. In the fall, though, temperatures along the lake will be a little bit warmer than in the rest of the state.

In January, Ohioans can expect the temperature to linger around 28 degrees Fahrenheit (–2 degrees Celsius) on average, which is just a little below freezing and perfect for snow. In July, warm, humid weather, with an average temperature of 73°F (23°C), hangs over the state. Ohioans spend the cold winter days snuggled in warm jackets and gloves from about November until March. They have warmer and stormier days, with thunderstorms and sometimes tornadoes possible, in the spring and summer. In the fall, the days are crisp and cool.

The wettest part of the state is located in the southwest around Wilmington. Toledo and Sandusky, in the northern part of the state, receive the least amount of rain and snow. People who live in northeastern Ohio see the most snow—almost 100 inches (254 centimeters) a year.

Ohio's lowest recorded temperature was –39°F (–39°C), which was measured in 1899 in Milligan, near New Lexington. The highest temperature was 113°F (45°C), recorded in Gallipolis in 1934.

Wildlife

When the first white settlers arrived in Ohio, forests covered much of the state, but early settlers cleared many trees to make way for farms and towns. Today, forests cover about one-fourth of Ohio. Forest trees include buckeyes, sycamores, maples, and oaks.

A wide range of flowers and trees grow in Ohio's forests, plains, and fields. Some of these plants produce things people can eat. The shagbark hickory tree, for example, produces nuts. This hickory tree is also the source for delicious syrup. Native Americans used to make a refreshing drink from the berries of the red sumac shrub. A tree that produces a fruit called a pawpaw grows in the river valleys of Ohio. Similar to a banana, the pawpaw is long and ripens to a brown color. In 2009, the pawpaw became the state's official native fruit.

The pawpaw, which grows in river valleys, is Ohio's official native fruit.

The state is also home to a variety of animals. Different types of birds, such as cardinals, chickadees, and sparrows, fly through the Ohio skies and nest in fields and trees. Cardinals, which generally do not live in thick forests, actually became much more common as forests were cleared. Fish, amphibians, and other aquatic animals live in Ohio's lakes, rivers, and streams. Ohio has snakes, turtles, salamanders, and frogs. Many of its woodland animals are small. In the forests are woodland creatures such as white-tailed deer, raccoons, opossums, squirrels, bats, and rabbits. Larger animals, such as wolves, cougars, bison, and elk, once filled Ohio's large wilderness areas, but their numbers decreased as more people moved into the area.

The black bear, for example, lived throughout the state at one time. By the 1850s, however, there were no black bears left in Ohio. Black bear populations are coming back because many regions are restoring their forests. Scientists recently counted more than one hundred black bears in Ohio, and some of them were females with cubs.

Bald eagles are also making a comeback. In 1979, the state had only four nesting pairs. Today, it has more than two hundred. Bald eagles were **endangered** at one point, due in part to habitat loss and pesticide use. (When a type of animal is endangered, there are so few left that the animal is at risk of becoming extinct, or completely dying out.)

Diverse Wildlife

Ohio's climate varies depending on your location in the state. As a result, you can find plants and animals in some parts of the state but not others. The common wall lizard, found often in Cincinnati, is one example of a subtropical animal that makes its home in the state.

Pesticides—chemicals that kill insects—eventually wash into the rivers and lakes and contaminate fish. Bald eagles eat the fish and are poisoned by the pesticides. Since many of the most dangerous pesticides are banned today, the health of the fish and the bald eagles is improving.

Like bald eagles, beavers were once numerous in what is now Ohio. In the 1700s and early 1800s, however, trappers could earn a great deal of money selling

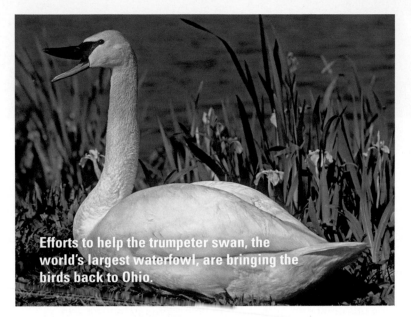
Efforts to help the trumpeter swan, the world's largest waterfowl, are bringing the birds back to Ohio.

beaver skins, and huge numbers of beavers were killed. By 1830, there were few beavers left. As beaver skins decreased in popularity, Ohio's beaver population began to increase. By the 1970s, it was estimated that more than five thousand beavers lived in Ohio. Scientists today believe that the beaver population has increased to more than twenty-five thousand.

Endangered Wildlife in Ohio

Ohio has several species of plants and animals that are considered endangered. Many things threaten wildlife, including human settlement that removes habitat, pesticides, overhunting, and pollution.

Several bird species, including the sandhill crane, the common tern, the golden-winged warbler, and the trumpeter swan, are on the state's list of endangered animals. The trumpeter swan is white with a black beak. It is the world's largest waterfowl. Hunted for food and feathers, trumpeter swan populations had practically disappeared by the early 1900s. By the mid-1900s, some programs to restore the trumpeter swan in the United States and Canada began. In 1996, Ohio joined a group of states that raised trumpeter swans in zoos and released several pairs into the wild. Today, the state has about seventy pairs of trumpeter swans.

The list of endangered species in Ohio also includes mammals such as the Indiana bat, plants like the running buffalo clover, and insects such as the American burying beetle.

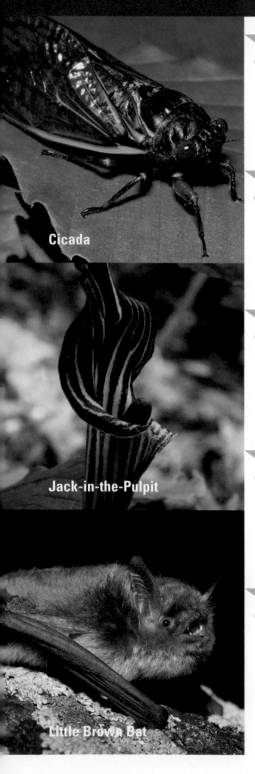

Cicada

Jack-in-the-Pulpit

Little Brown Bat

1. Cicada

Many Ohioans call this insect a locust, but cicadas and locusts belong to different families of insects. The male cicada produces a mating call by vibrating its drumlike abdomen to attract females.

2. Jack-in-the-Pulpit

This uniquely named plant has large, glossy leaves and distinctive hooded flowers. In late summer, it sprouts a cluster of bright red berries. The plant is considered a tuber and can be eaten if dried or cooked.

3. Little Brown Bat

The little brown bat is one of thirteen bat species found in Ohio. Recently, the population of this bat has declined, causing them to be placed on a list of "species of concern." State officials are investigating the decline.

4. Perch

The yellow perch, native to Ohio, can be found in lakes, ponds, and slow-moving rivers. This fish, which is golden yellow with black stripes, prefers clear water with a sandy bottom. It is also known as lake or raccoon perch.

5. Persimmon Tree

Native to Ohio, the persimmon tree grows in the southern part of the state. Because persimmon wood is very hard, it is used by businesses that produce wood heads for golf clubs and cue sticks for billiards.

6. Red-Tailed Hawk

These large birds have broad wings and a short, fan-shaped tail that helps them soar for long periods. Red-tailed hawks are not endangered, but it is illegal to hunt them because of their important role—controlling the number of small mammals—in the ecosystem.

7. Scarlet Carnation

Ohio native President William McKinley wore a carnation in his lapel for luck during his political career. After McKinley was assassinated in 1901, the Ohio legislature honored him by making the scarlet carnation the state flower in 1904.

8. Trillium

The trillium is Ohio's state wildflower. It has three large ruffled petals and three large oval leaves. Its name comes from the Latin word for "three." Trillium is found throughout Ohio in the early spring.

9. Weasel

Weasels live throughout the United States, but their numbers are especially high in Ohio. Weasels live in forests and on Ohio farmlands, as long as there is water nearby. Catching and eating mice is one of the weasel's specialties.

10. White Trout Lily

This plant is a perennial, meaning it returns every year. Each plant produces a single white flower with curved petals. The white trout lily can spread and produce large colonies if left undisturbed.

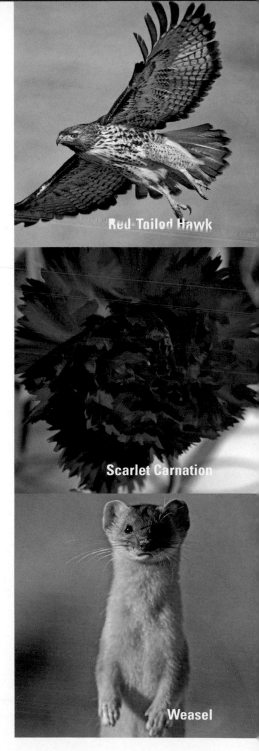

Red-Tailed Hawk

Scarlet Carnation

Weasel

The open mouth of a snake can be seen in this aerial view of Serpent Mound, which is 1,330 feet (405 m) long.

From the Beginning

cientists and historians estimate that people have lived in what is now Ohio for about fifteen thousand years. The first people, called Paleo-Indians, inhabited Ohio during the last Ice Age. Paleo-Indians moved from place to place, hunting wild animals, fishing, and gathering fruits and nuts. They used **flint**, an important natural resource from the area, to make tools and weapons. "Paleo" means ancient.

Over time, thick forests started to grow as warming climates melted glaciers. Continuing in the tradition of their Paleo-Indian ancestors, the Archaic people hunted and gathered food. Unlike the Paleo-Indians, however, they settled down in permanent camps. They, too, mined flint and other stones to make axes used to cut down trees, build canoes, and create decorative ornaments for spears.

Mound Builders

The Woodland period started in today's Ohio about three thousand years ago. During this period, hunting and gathering shifted to farming. Prehistoric people started to settle into more permanent villages, create pottery, harvest crops, and build elaborate mounds with raised piles of earth and stone. The mounds, often constructed in the shape of animals and geometric figures, were used to bury the dead and other treasured items.

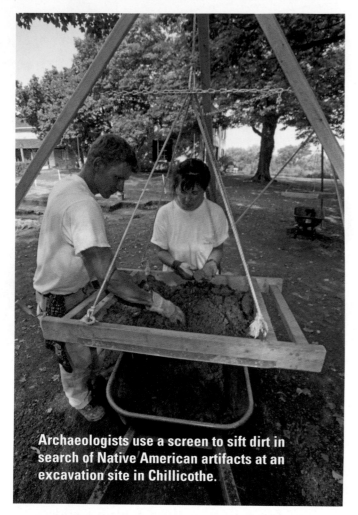

Archaeologists use a screen to sift dirt in search of Native American artifacts at an excavation site in Chillicothe.

The first of these Woodland groups was the Adena. The Adena people were the area's first farmers. They grew crops such as squash and sunflowers. Because they needed to tend their various crops, the Adena people built small, permanent villages.

Located in Adams County in southern Ohio, Serpent Mound is the largest mound in the United States. It is likely that the Fort Ancient people built it more than one thousand years ago. Resembling a huge snake, Serpent Mound is 1,330 feet (405 m) long, and visitors can see the serpent's open jaws at one end.

Another Woodland group of skilled mound builders, called the Hopewell, lived in the area about 1,500 years ago. They built gigantic mounds of various shapes that enclosed hundreds of acres of land. The Hopewell lived in small villages where they grew crops, fished, hunted wild game, and gathered plants. They were also superior traders. They obtained shells from the Gulf of Mexico, copper from the Great Lakes region, and a mineral called mica from the Carolinas. Many of the mounds built by the Hopewell have been found intact by archaeologists and provide great insight into the culture of this group. Burial mounds were discovered containing exotic goods that gave historians clues to the **hierarchy**, or structure, of the Hopewell. Among the best examples of these discoveries are the burial mounds found in the Ohio town of Chillicothe. Archaeologists consider Ohio to be one of the most important locations for discoveries related to the Hopewell.

From 600 CE to 1200 CE, the culture began to change. Villages grew larger, and many communities began to surround themselves with a defensive wall or ditch for protection. During this time, an important innovation—the bow and arrow—was used for hunting and as a weapon. While the Woodland people still cultivated squash and sunflowers, they began to grow corn, or maize, around 800 CE. Included among the last groups who inhabited the land until the seventeenth century were the Fort Ancient people in southern Ohio, the Sandusky in northwestern Ohio, and the Whittlesey in northeastern Ohio.

The Iroquois

During the 1600s, the powerful Iroquois, from the area of present-day New York, made their way into the region. The Iroquois peoples (members of a confederacy of several tribes) came in search of new hunting grounds, and they found an abundance of wildlife and edible plants in what is now Ohio. As a result, they pushed out most of the descendants of Ohio's prehistoric Native American cultures.

By the 1700s, as the Iroquois grew less powerful in what is now Ohio, other Native American groups began to move into the area. One tribe, the Huron, moved south from Canada and settled around the Sandusky River. Another Native American group, the Miami people, came from the west. They set up villages along the rivers that now bear their name—the Great Miami and the Little Miami. Some bands of Iroquois also first moved to Ohio around this time. The Mingo were a small group of Native Americans related to the Iroquois. They left the Iroquois homeland in the New York area and settled mostly in eastern and central Ohio. The Lenape people, also called the Delaware, settled in eastern Ohio. The Shawnee, who were pushed out of Pennsylvania by white settlers, moved into southern Ohio.

This engraving shows Native Americans meeting with French military leaders on the banks of the Muskingum River.

French and English Control

European exploration of the land that is now Ohio began in the mid-1600s. René-Robert Cavelier, sieur de La Salle, a French explorer from Canada, was likely the first European to set foot in what is now Ohio. La Salle is believed to have explored the Ohio River as early as 1669. Based on his travels, France claimed the region, but England also believed it had a right to the land, which it considered the western extent of its Atlantic-coast colonies.

The Native People

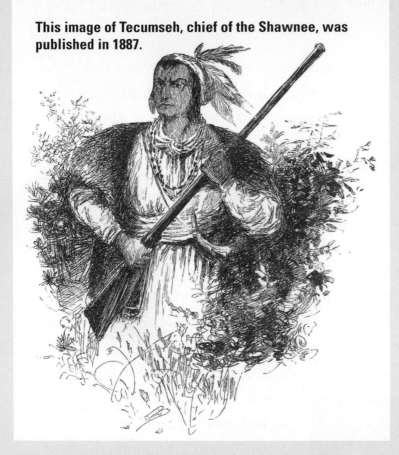

This image of Tecumseh, chief of the Shawnee, was published in 1887.

Native Americans have played an important role in Ohio's cultural landscape for centuries. The original tribes in the area were the Erie, Kickapoo, and Shawnee. Many tribes from other regions were forced to migrate to Ohio after European settlers arrived on the continent. They were the Lenape (Delaware), Miami, Ottawa, Ohio Seneca, and Huron (Wyandot) tribes.

Most of the original tribes in the Ohio area spoke a version of the Algonquian language. They lived largely in permanent homes in villages, and their food source was based on farming. The kinds of houses they lived in were varied. Many lived in domed houses. The Miami tribe lived in oval houses with walls made of woven reeds. They also hunted animals like deer using a bow and arrow, tomahawks, and spears. The Shawnee people were different from most of the surrounding tribes, as they were a migratory people who lived in scattered villages across the region and moved frequently from place to place. Many Native Americans in this area wore clothing made out of animal hide. The men wore **breechcloths** and the women wore skirts and leggings. Beads and feathers were sometimes used to decorate clothing, especially items used for special occasions or ceremonies.

European settlers made an impact on Ohio's Native people before they even arrived in the region. When Native Americans from other areas were forced to move there, they brought European diseases like smallpox that **decimated**, or nearly wiped out, the Native population already living there. Most of the Native Americans who were living in the region originally either joined other tribes or moved to different areas, including the southern portion of the United States, after the Europeans arrived. Most of the remaining Native Americans were forced to relocate during the 1800s.

Today, there are no federally recognized tribes in Ohio. The tribes are not extinct, but most of them moved to other parts of the country. Many Ohio Native Americans, particularly those who were members of the Shawnee and Miami tribes, moved to Oklahoma. There is still a small but proud group of Native Americans from these tribes living in Oklahoma today.

Spotlight on the Shawnee

The name of the Shawnee people comes from the Shawnee word shawanwa, meaning "southerner."

Distribution: Most of the Shawnee people originally lived in Ohio, Kentucky, and Indiana. Their migratory status means that Shawnee people could once be found in places as far-flung as New York and Georgia. Today, most Shawnee live in Oklahoma.

Food: Like many other Native Americans in the region, the Shawnee were farmers. The women in the tribe were in charge of the farming and harvesting, and would raise corn, squash, beans, and other crops. Shawnee men hunted deer, turkeys, and other small animals in the forest. They also fished in rivers and lakes. Soups, stews, and cornbread were important dishes to the Shawnee.

Homes: The Shawnee lived in villages made up of small round houses called wigwams. Wigwams usually had wood frames and were covered in birch bark. Each village also had a larger council house made of wood where tribal leaders could gather.

Clothes: Shawnee clothes were made of animal hide and other materials found in nature. Women wore skirts and leggings, and men wore breechcloths and leggings. In cold weather, both men and women wore ponchos to stay warm. Shawnee people wore moccasins on their feet. Some wore headbands decorated with beads and feathers.

Artwork: The Shawnee people were known for their beadwork, pottery, and woodcarving. They also made wampum, artwork featuring white and purple beads made from shells. The designs on wampum belts often told a story or represented a family's history.

For the next century, the French and the English fought over the right to claim the land referred to as the Ohio Country. This region included most of what would become Ohio, as well as portions of Indiana, West Virginia, and Pennsylvania. Both the French and the English set up fur-trading companies in the region. Both wanted to control the profitable trade in the animal skins that Native Americans brought to trading posts. Both tried to convince different Native American groups to join them in their wars.

The final clash in this ongoing conflict between France and Great Britain was the French and Indian War (1754–1763). Britain won the war and the right to claim all of the Ohio Country (as well as almost all the rest of North America east of the Mississippi River).

The Northwest Territory

After Britain won the French and Indian War, it tried to prevent American colonists from moving west into the Ohio Country. Britain wanted good relations with the region's

George Washington fought on the side of the British in the Ohio Country during the French and Indian War.

Native American groups in order to avoid costly wars and to protect its fur trade. Not many years after, however, war broke out between the American colonists and Britain. During the American Revolution (1775–1783), the American colonists fought for independence from Britain.

After the colonists won the American Revolution, the United States was formed, and Britain gave up its claim to the Ohio Country. In 1787, the United States organized the vast region northwest of the Ohio River into the Northwest Territory. This large area of frontier land included the present-day states of Ohio, Indiana, Illinois, Michigan, and Wisconsin, as well as part of Minnesota.

On July 13, 1787, the Northwest Ordinance was passed. This document outlined how the Northwest Territory was to be divided and governed. The Northwest Ordinance ultimately paved the way for Ohio to become the seventeenth state. According to the document, the US Congress selected the first governor. As soon as five thousand male landowners lived in the territory, they could elect their own legislature, which included a house of representatives and a legislative council. Later, when sixty thousand people lived in one portion of the territory, that portion could apply for statehood.

American settlers were eager to move into the Northwest Territory. In 1788, pioneers from New England, led by General Rufus Putnam, founded Marietta, the first permanent settlement by people of European descent north and west of the Ohio River. Marietta (named after France's Queen Marie Antoinette) was declared the first capital of the Northwest Territory. General Arthur St. Clair was appointed governor of the Northwest Territory.

Battle of Fallen Timbers

As Americans from the East settled the Northwest Territory in larger and larger numbers, the region's Native Americans fought to keep their land. After several victories, in 1794, they suffered a terrible defeat at the Battle of Fallen Timbers, near present-day Toledo. The area got its name from trees that had been knocked down by a tornado. General "Mad Anthony" Wayne led an army of three thousand troops in the battle. The Native American forces were led by a commander named Blue Jacket and made up of members of the

Making a Buckeye Wreath

Gather buckeyes from your neighborhood and hang this wreath in your home to show your Ohio pride. If you can't find buckeyes outside, try your local grocery or craft store. Chestnuts or horse chestnuts are very similar and can be used as well.

What You Need

A sturdy plastic plate or
    Styrofoam ring
Several (about 2–3 cups)
    buckeyes or chestnuts
Scissors
Glue (A hot glue gun works well;
    ask a grown-up for help)
Brown crepe paper (if using
    a ring)
Acorns, pine cones, walnuts, or
    leaves (optional)
Bows, glitter, yarn, paint, or other decorative items (optional)

What To Do

- Use the scissors to cut the inner circle out of the paper plate so you are left with a wreath shape. You may need a grown-up's help for this. Discard the inner circle part. If using a Styrofoam ring, wrap in brown crepe paper.

- Place a small amount of glue on each buckeye and glue it to the plate or ring. Place the buckeyes close together so you can't see the plate behind them.

- Continue until buckeyes cover as much of the plate as possible.

- Glue the pine cones, acorns, or leaves onto the wreath around the buckeyes to decorate it.

- Add the glitter, bow, paint or other decorative items in any way you like.

- Allow the wreath to sit for about 30 minutes so it dries completely.

- Once dry, display your wreath with pride! Ask an adult for help if you want to hang it on the wall.

Native Americans were forced to give up most of their land in Ohio after their defeat at the Battle of Fallen Timbers.

Shawnee, Lenape, Miami, Ottawa, and other tribes. As American forces closed in, the Native Americans fled toward a British **outpost** called Fort Miami, but British forces were unwilling to help them because they wanted to avoid a war with the Americans. Afterward, Native American tribes signed the Treaty of Greenville in 1795, giving up most of their lands in Ohio. Additionally, news of the American victory helped convince the British to withdraw from their forts in the area. General Wayne led the construction of American forts in the area, starting in present-day Toledo.

Statehood

By 1803, the eastern portion of the Northwest Territory had enough residents for Ohio to apply for statehood. On March 1, 1803, Ohio became the seventeenth US state. It was the first state carved out of the territory.

Ohio's first capital was Chillicothe. Zanesville was made the capital in 1810, but two years later, the legislature returned the capital to Chillicothe. Then, in 1816, Columbus was chosen as Ohio's permanent state capital. The capital was named after explorer Christopher Columbus.

Moses Cleaveland of Connecticut founded Cleveland in 1796. According to one legend, the local newspaper at the time dropped the "a" from Cleaveland's name to fit it in a headline.

In 1953, Ohio congressman George Bender introduced legislation to make Ohio a state after it was discovered that the state's constitution had never officially

In Their Own Words

"It is easy to pronounce, is pleasant in sound, and there is no other city of that name on the American continent." —Merchant Willard J. Daniels, on how Toledo was named

Shawnee chief Tecumseh died in battle while fighting to keep settlers from taking land from Native American tribes.

Tecumseh.

been **ratified** in 1803. Technically, Ohio was still part of the Northwest Territory due to this legislative mistake. On May 19, 1953, the House voted to approve legislation retroactively ratifying the state constitution and admitting Ohio to the Union as of March 1, 1803.

Native American Losses

Although Ohio was now a state, tensions between white settlers and Native Americans continued. By the 1800s, many Native American groups were suffering. More and more of their land was being taken over by white settlers, and hunting for the fur trade had caused animal populations to dwindle. Many Native Americans had trouble finding food.

Native American leaders were concerned about their people and the loss of their land. Shawnee chief Tecumseh and his brother, known as the Prophet, tried to unite many tribes to stop white settlers from taking their land. General William Henry Harrison, who later became president of the United States, knew of Tecumseh's plans. In 1811, Harrison's troops attacked and destroyed Prophetstown, the largest Shawnee village (located in present-day Indiana). This defeat, in what became known as the Battle of Tippecanoe, seriously weakened Tecumseh and his followers, but he did not give up.

In an attempt to defeat General Harrison and regain Ohio's lands, Tecumseh and his men joined forces with the British army against the Americans when the War of 1812 (1812–1815) began. Tecumseh hoped that if the British won, they would return the land to the Native Americans.

The United States fought Great Britain for control of Lake Erie during the War of 1812. In 1813, US ships commanded by Lieutenant Oliver Hazard Perry won the Battle of Lake Erie, which was fought off Ohio's shores. The victory paved the way for General Harrison

Commander Oliver Perry transfers to the brig *Niagara* after his flagship was damaged during the American victory in the Battle of Lake Erie in 1813.

to cross Lake Erie and successfully attack British and Native American forces at the Battle of the Thames in Canada in 1813. Tecumseh was killed during the fighting. The US victory essentially marked the end of the alliance among Native American tribes that Tecumseh had worked to create.

A monument to Perry (1785–1819) was erected on the Ohio Island of Put-in-Bay in Lake Erie. Hazard earned the title "Hero of Lake Erie" for leading American forces in a naval victory over the British in the Battle of Lake Erie during the War of 1812.

The New State Grows

After Ohio became a state, its government encouraged settlers to move into the area. Ohio grew quickly during the nineteenth century. By 1860, more than two million people lived in Ohio, making it the country's third-most-populous state. Many Ohioans were farmers, who grew crops such as corn, beans, and melons, and raised livestock. Farmers also planted apple and peach orchards and shipped the fruit to the East Coast. They planted tobacco, which was manufactured into smoking materials. Factories were built to process Ohio's crops. Other factories began producing farm equipment, such as tractors and reapers.

Improvements in transportation helped farming businesses, too. Paved roads made it easier to transport crops to the East Coast. The development of steamboats in the early 1800s helped to deliver products quickly to the South by way of the Mississippi River.

10 KEY CITIES ★ ★

1. Columbus: population 787,033

Columbus was founded in 1812 as the state's capital. Manufacturing and steel were once key parts of Columbus's economy. Today, it has a diverse economy based on education, banking, aviation, health care, energy, and a number of other thriving industries.

2. Cleveland: population 396,815

Ohio's second most populous city is located in the northeastern portion of the state on the shores of Lake Erie. Cleveland was founded in 1796 on the Cuyahoga River. For years, the center of its economy was manufacturing.

3. Cincinnati: population 296,943

Cincinnati was the first city founded after the American Revolutionary War ended. For much of the nineteenth century, it was one of the ten largest cities by population in the United States. It is known for its beautiful architecture.

4. Toledo: population 287,208

Toledo was established in 1833. It grew and thrived quickly because of its location on the Miami and Erie Canal. Toledo has a long history of innovation in the glass industry, earning it the nickname "the Glass City."

5. Akron: population 199,110

In the early twentieth century, Akron became known as the Rubber Capital of the World because it was home to four major tire companies: Goodrich, Goodyear, Firestone, and General Tire. The city has many research and technology facilities.

Columbus

Akron

OHIO ★ ★ ★ ★ ★ ★

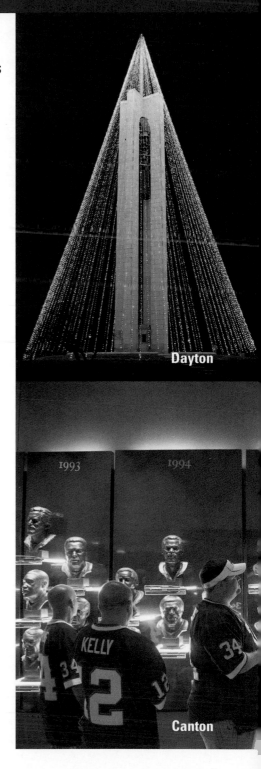

6. Dayton: population 141,527

Dayton's economy is supported by new technology companies in aerospace, defense, and other industries. Many inventors were raised in Dayton, including Orville Wright, who helped invent the airplane. Health care is another thriving industry.

7. Parma: population 81,601

Many people who work in Cleveland live in nearby Parma because of its high quality of life. In 2014, Parma was ranked as the third safest city in the nation among cities with a population of 25,000 or more.

8. Canton: population 73,007

Canton is a favorite of many football fans, as it is home to the Pro Football Hall of Fame. The organization that would become the National Football League was formed there. It is also where President William McKinley lived as an adult.

9. Youngstown: population 66,982

Youngstown's thriving coal and steel industry in the early twentieth century attracted immigrants from many places, including Italy, Greece, and what are today Lebanon, Palestine and Israel, and Syria. Today, the largest employer in the city is Youngstown State University.

10. Lorain: population 64,097

On June 28, 1924, a tornado struck the city of Lorain and nearby Sandusky. Many buildings in downtown Lorain were damaged, but the recovery process included constructing several notable buildings that still stand.

Dayton

Canton

Canals were dug in Ohio in the first half of the nineteenth century to connect bodies of water and improve trade.

The building of canals also helped Ohio expand its industry and transport its goods. Workers dug the long, narrow waterways so that boats could travel over hilly terrain. In 1832, the Ohio and Erie Canal was completed, connecting Cleveland on Lake Erie and Portsmouth on the Ohio River. In 1845, the Miami and Ohio Canal opened. It connected Toledo and Cincinnati. Although canals brought many benefits to Ohio and strengthened the state's economy and trade industries, they were imperfect means of travel. Flooding and, during cold Ohio winters, freezing could do damage to the canals and surrounding areas. In the northern half of the state, canals were generally drained during the winter so workers could repair any damage. The southern part of the state did not usually face the same problems. These difficulties contributed in part to the eventual decline of canal use and the need for other means of moving goods, such as railroads.

By the 1850s, railroads had become the latest improvement in transportation. They contributed to the decline of canals. Trains became a quick, cheap way to move Ohio's products throughout the country. By the 1900s, most of the canals were no longer in use.

Agriculture remained a strong industry in Ohio until the late nineteenth century. By then, other states in the West had been admitted to the Union, and Ohio farmers had trouble competing with their low prices. Many Ohioans sold their farms and moved to the thriving cities to find other types of work. Cleveland, which began as a frontier outpost, expanded into a major industrial hub. Cincinnati became the country's largest meatpacking center, earning it the nickname "Porkopolis."

Ancient Greeks played the game of quoits (pronounced KWOITZ) more than two thousand years ago. A form of the game eventually became popular among English colonists, who brought it with them to North America. In Ohio and other states, the game of quoits developed into horseshoes.

Slavery and the Civil War

As Ohioans were getting used to life in their new state, the country faced a serious conflict between Northern states and Southern states over the issue of slavery. As a Free State, Ohio did not allow slavery. By the early 1800s, most Northern states no longer allowed, or were in the process of ending, the practice of slavery. Millions of people, descendants of Africans captured and forcibly brought to the Americas, were slaves in the Southern states. A very strong antislavery movement developed in Ohio in the decades before the Civil War (1861–1865). Ohio resident Harriet Beecher Stowe wrote the famous antislavery book *Uncle Tom's Cabin*, which was published in 1852.

Many enslaved people in the South tried to escape to freedom by heading to Canada. They often traveled through Ohio, where there were many abolitionists, or people who

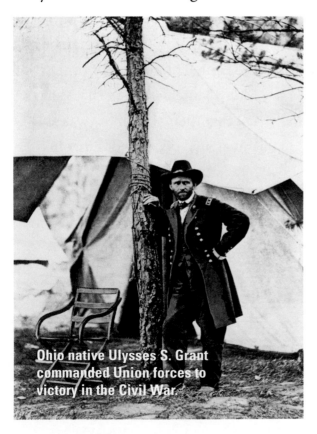

Ohio native Ulysses S. Grant commanded Union forces to victory in the Civil War.

wanted to get rid of slavery. Ohioans helped slaves escape along the Underground Railroad. This was not an actual railroad but a secret network of people and hiding places that helped runaway slaves travel to freedom. People who disagreed with slavery hid runaway slaves in their homes. They fed, clothed, and cared for them before sending them on the next leg of their journey.

The Rankin House in Ripley, Ohio, was a famous hiding place on the Underground Railroad. From 1825 to 1865, Presbyterian minister John Rankin and his wife provided shelter to more than two thousand escaped slaves. The home is currently a museum run by the Ohio Historical Society.

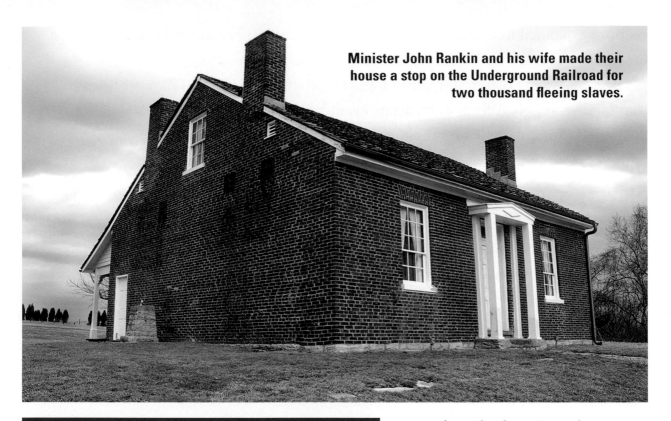

Minister John Rankin and his wife made their house a stop on the Underground Railroad for two thousand fleeing slaves.

Cincinnati's Civil War Role

Cincinnati played an important role in the Civil War for several reasons. A large amount of supplies and equipment, including gunboats, armor plating, and cannons, were manufactured there. It was also a major traveling path for escaped slaves coming over the border from Kentucky.

After Abraham Lincoln was elected president in 1860, eleven Southern states seceded from, or left, the Union (another name for the United States at that time). Many white people in these states felt that their way of life was threatened because of Lincoln's opposition to slavery. By the spring of 1861, the Civil War had begun.

During the war, about 345,000 Ohioans fought for the North, the most famous of whom was Ulysses S. Grant, who eventually became the commander of all Union armies.

Union forces defeated the South in 1865. After the war ended, the Thirteenth Amendment to the US Constitution was adopted, which outlawed slavery throughout the United States.

Political and Industrial Might

After the end of the Civil War, Ohio residents became active leaders in politics and industry. From 1869 to 1881, Ohio sent three of its natives to the White House.

US presidents from Ohio who served during this time included Ulysses S. Grant, Rutherford B. Hayes, and James Garfield. In 1870, John D. Rockefeller opened the Standard Oil Company of Ohio, which within a decade owned almost all the country's oil refineries. In 1879, Charles Brush demonstrated his arc streetlights in Cleveland, making it the first city in the country to light its streets using electricity.

Construction began on Ohio's first railroad in 1835 and was completed by 1836. It connected Toledo, Ohio, to Adrian, Michigan, and covered a distance of 33 miles (53 km). The trip took three hours.

Just before the end of the nineteenth century, the Goodyear Tire and Rubber Company opened in Akron. The company was named after Charles Goodyear, who in 1844 developed vulcanization, the process that gives rubber strength. Goodyear manufactured rubber products, such as tires, tubes, and hoses, and it eventually became the nation's largest tire company.

Economic Turmoil

Ohio cities prospered at the beginning of the twentieth century. Tall skyscrapers and other modern office buildings were built. By the 1920s, Cleveland was the fifth-largest city in the United States.

However, in the 1930s, Ohio suffered from the effects of the **Great Depression** (1929–1939). During this difficult economic period, jobs were scarce and many people suffered greatly. Until then, Ohio had been one of the leading industrial states. It was a tough time for Ohio and the rest of the country. The US government set up programs that hired unemployed workers to build roads, dams, and other projects.

World War II

Another major event helped bring economic recovery to Ohio. World War II (1939–1945) was a global conflict, and American soldiers and their allies needed food and military equipment. The United States joined the war in 1941 after Japan bombed the US Navy

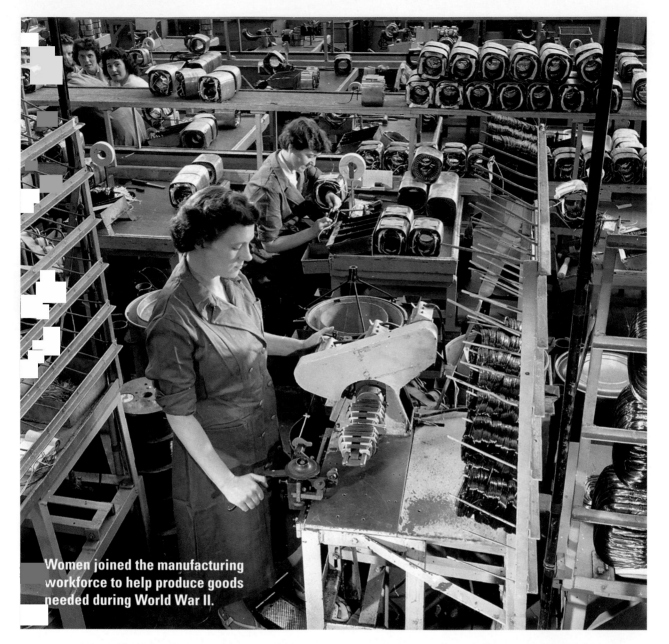

Women joined the manufacturing workforce to help produce goods needed during World War II.

base at Pearl Harbor in Hawaii. Nearly 840,000 Ohioans served in the armed forces. On the home front, women entered the workforce, filling jobs in factories that produced steel, weapons, and aircraft.

After the war, industries continued to grow and more people poured into the state. Cities became so crowded that developers began buying the land around the cities to build homes, and suburbs developed. At this same time, new interstate highways provided quicker routes from one major city to another. By the 1960s, Ohio was one of the most populated states.

Four students died when members of the National Guard fired at Vietnam War protesters on the Kent State campus.

A Time of Protests

The 1960s were also a time of turmoil for much of the country. African Americans sought greater equality during the civil rights movement. Sometimes, however, protests turned violent in several major cities, including Cleveland.

At the same time, Americans debated the country's involvement in the Vietnam War. Many Americans opposed the war. In May 1970, perhaps the most famous Vietnam War protest took place at Kent State University, near Akron. During the antiwar demonstration, National Guardsmen fatally shot four students and wounded nine others. The tragedy made national headlines and increased support for the antiwar movement.

The Decision

Cleveland Cavaliers star forward LeBron James made many loyal fans mad in 2010 when he announced his decision to leave the team to play for the Miami Heat. The Akron native made the announcement in a highly-viewed ESPN special called "The Decision." He returned to the Cavaliers in 2014.

The New Millennium and Beyond

Ohio's large industries improved the economy, but the state's factories also polluted the environment. The plants and animals in Lake Erie were dying from toxic waste being dumped into the water. Then, in 1969, a portion of the Cuyahoga River in Cleveland was so full of chemicals that it actually caught fire. Ohioans realized they had many serious environmental issues to face. Since then, Ohioans have voted to help pay for projects to improve the natural environment. Their efforts have proven successful in many ways. In both Lake Erie and the Cuyahoga River, pollution levels have been substantially reduced.

During the 1980s and 1990s, modern industries began to gain prominence in the state. Computers, automobiles, paper products, and machinery became some of Ohio's top economic drivers.

Today, Ohio finds itself in a time of transition. Once one of the leading industrial giants in the United States, by the early twenty-first century the state had lost many factories as a result of economic failure or relocation to other states and other countries. People dependent on manufacturing jobs for their livelihood often found such jobs to be harder to get. This situation became worse with the onset of difficult economic times that hit the country beginning in late 2007. Like the rest of the United States, Ohio faced one of the toughest economic crises since the Great Depression. With a long and well-preserved history, however, Ohioans know how to face challenges and work to come out ahead.

10 KEY DATES IN STATE HISTORY

 1. July 6, 1669

Frenchman René-Robert Cavelier, sieur de La Salle, begins his explorations of large portions of what would become the northeastern United States, including the Ohio River.

 2. April 7, 1788

Marietta is established. It is the first permanent settlement by people of European descent in present-day Ohio, then part of the Northwest Territory.

 3. February 19, 1803

President Thomas Jefferson signs an act of Congress to approve Ohio's boundaries and constitution. The General Assembly meets for the first time on March 1. This is the day Ohio celebrates becoming the seventeenth state.

 4. July 4, 1827

The first span of the Ohio and Erie Canal is opened, stretching between Akron and Cleveland. The full canal is completed in 1832.

 5. May 4, 1869

The Cincinnati Red Stockings, later the Cincinnati Reds, play their first game as the nation's first professional baseball team. The team had ten players.

 6. September 7, 1963

The Pro Football Hall of Fame and Museum opens in Canton. Seventeen players are inducted the first year.

 7. July 20, 1969

Neil Armstrong, born in Wapakoneta, becomes the first person to walk on the moon. An estimated six hundred million people watch the event on television.

 8. September 2, 1995

The Rock and Roll Hall of Fame and Museum opens in Cleveland with a concert that includes Bob Dylan, Aretha Franklin, and others.

 9. June 4, 2010

Ohio teen Anamika Veeramani wins the Scripps National Spelling Bee by correctly spelling the word "stromuhr."

 10. July 21, 2015

Ohio governor John Kasich announces he is running for president in the 2016 election, becoming the sixteenth Republican to join the race. He wins the Ohio primary in April 2016.

Members of the West Side Irish American Club in Cleveland celebrate St. Patrick's Day.

The People

Ohio's population has grown over the centuries. In 1800, just three years before Ohio officially became a state, a little more than forty-five thousand people lived there. As industries boomed in Ohio, so did the population. In 1860, more than 2.4 million people resided in Ohio, making it the third-most-populous state, behind New York and Pennsylvania. By 1900, the population reached 4.2 million people. Fifty years later, close to 8 million people called Ohio home. According to the 2010 census, Ohio has a little more than 11.5 million residents. Today, the state population is the seventh largest in the country.

So where exactly do all these Ohioans come from? People of many different nationalities and cultures make up the Buckeye State.

Native Americans

Native Americans were the first people to populate present-day Ohio. Remains of ancient cultures have provided scientists with enough information for them to guess that people lived in this area at least fifteen thousand years ago. Most of these early people were constantly moving to find food. They survived on their skills as hunters.

By the seventeenth and eighteenth centuries, the largest Native American groups in what is now Ohio included the Iroquois, Shawnee, Lenape, and Miami. Many of these

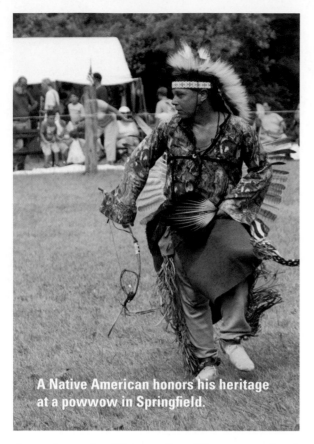
A Native American honors his heritage at a powwow in Springfield.

people lived in permanent villages near rivers and streams, for access to fresh water. For food, they hunted and also raised crops. While people were on hunting expeditions, a tent called a tepee gave protection from bad weather.

As white settlers moved into the region, Native Americans found their way of life threatened. Although they tried to unite to protect their land and homes, they were unsuccessful. Some Native Americans had to move to reservation land in Ohio. By the late 1800s, all reservations in Ohio were closed. Most Native Americans were forced to move to reservations in other states.

The **US Census Bureau** estimates there are fewer than twenty-six thousand Native Americans in Ohio today. They attend school, work, and enjoy the lifestyle that their state offers. Many still practice their traditions. Annual festivals and other gatherings give Ohio's Native Americans opportunities to celebrate their history and heritage.

The Europeans

The French were the first Europeans to come to the Ohio area. Most of them were fur trappers, fur traders, or missionaries who came to convert the Native Americans to Christianity. After the British won the French and Indian War, they claimed the land that would become Ohio, until the American Revolution. Some former British soldiers settled permanently in the area. After the Revolution, many Americans of English descent began settling in the region.

Today, many Ohioans trace their ancestry back to Europe. Some share the heritage of the early pioneering settlers. Later, people began immigrating to Ohio from throughout Europe.

During the 1840s, people from Ireland came to the United States to escape the Irish potato **famine**. The failure of the important potato crops caused more than a million people in Ireland to die from starvation and related illnesses. Prejudice against Irish workers, mostly because of their Catholic backgrounds, made it difficult for them to find jobs in the United States. Irish immigrants often had to take tough, poorly paid jobs, such

Making History in Education

George B. Vashon was the first African American to graduate from Oberlin College. Vashon went on to become the first black lawyer in New York, the third black person to hold a teaching position at a college or university, and the first black professor at Howard University.

as digging Ohio's canals and laying railroad tracks. Irish immigrants also clashed with newly-arrived freed slaves and other African-American residents. Despite these hardships, the Irish immigrants and their work ethic contributed greatly to the growth of the state. Because the Irish faced discrimination and conflict, they often established their own communities where they could continue practicing and celebrating their cultural heritage. Those cultural aspects are still celebrated in Ohio today, with social clubs like the West Side Irish American Club of Cleveland.

By 1850, almost half of Ohio's immigrant population came from Germany. Most Germans settled around Ohio's major cities. Some were skilled craftspeople who helped create some of Ohio's major buildings. Some cities in Ohio still have large German-American populations. In Cincinnati, for example, almost half of the city's population is descended from German immigrants. When these German immigrants first arrived in Cincinnati, most of them lived in a neighborhood called Over-the-Rhine. This and other predominantly German neighborhoods in the state often had German-speaking churches, clubs, and German language newspapers. Unfortunately, Germans were not always made to feel welcome in Cincinnati. In 1855, anti-German sentiment led to violence in the city.

Around 1900, many people in Ohio were of English, German, or Irish descent, but the population was about to become more diverse. By the late 1800s and early 1900s, Russians, Poles, Hungarians, Bulgarians, Croatians, Czechs, Slovaks, and people from other Eastern European areas began settling in Ohio's major cities. Immigrants from Italy and Greece also came in large numbers. So many people were moving to Ohio that, in the early 1900s, almost three-fourths of Cleveland's residents said either they or their parents were born outside the United States. Like the Germans and Irish, these immigrants also faced some discrimination from native Ohioans. Some local residents called for laws that would limit the traditional cultural practices of some immigrants. Fortunately, Eastern European immigrants maintained many aspects of their heritage and shared them with their new neighbors. They opened theater companies, newspapers, dance troupes, and other organizations. Many of these cultural contributions are still celebrated in Ohio today.

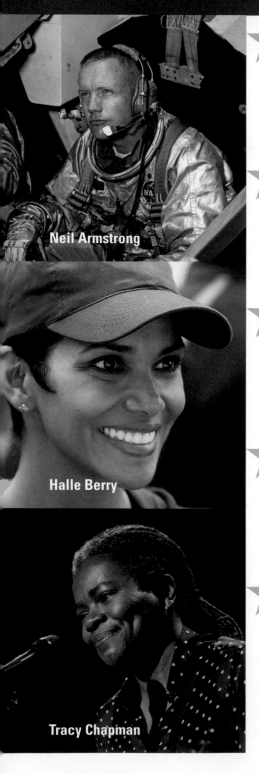

Neil Armstrong

Halle Berry

Tracy Chapman

1. Neil Armstrong

Born in 1930 in Wapakoneta, Armstrong was a pilot for the US Navy and later a professor of aerospace engineering. As a NASA astronaut, Armstrong became the first person to set foot on the moon, on July 20, 1969.

2. Halle Berry

In 1966, Halle Berry was born in Cleveland. In 2002, she made history as the first African-American woman to win the Academy Award for Best Actress. She is also famous for her role as Storm in the X-Men movies.

3. Drew Carey

Drew Carey was born in 1958 and raised in Cleveland. His television show *The Drew Carey Show* was set in his hometown and ran from 1995 to 2004. He also hosted *Whose Line Is It Anyway?* and *The Price is Right*.

4. Nancy Cartwright

Nancy Cartwright is a voice actor who was born in Dayton in 1957. Since 1989, she has been the voice of Bart Simpson on the Fox Network's *The Simpsons*. She also spoke the role of Chuckie on Nickelodeon's *Rugrats*.

5. Tracy Chapman

Singer Tracy Chapman was born in Cleveland in 1964. She gained fame for her 1988 single "Fast Car." Chapman has won four Grammy Awards over the course of her career, including one for another hit single, "Give Me One Reason."

6. John Legend

This singer-songwriter was born in Springfield in 1978. He has won nine Grammy Awards, one Golden Globe, and an Academy Award for his music. His 2014 single "All of Me" became one of the best-selling digital singles of all time.

7. Maya Lin

Maya Lin was born in 1959 in Athens. As a student at Yale University, she entered a national design competition for a memorial for Vietnam War veterans and won. The Vietnam Veterans Memorial in Washington, DC, was completed in 1982.

8. Annie Oakley

Born in Willowdell in 1860, Annie Oakley became known for her sharpshooting skills at the age of fifteen. She became world famous for her talent and accuracy in shooting a gun, even performing for Queen Victoria.

9. Jesse Owens

Born in 1913, Owens was eight years old when his family moved to Cleveland. He became one of the greatest track and field stars of all time. In 1976, President Gerald Ford gave Owens the Presidential Medal of Freedom.

10. Cy Young

Denton Young, born in 1867 in Gilmore, was an outstanding baseball pitcher for several professional teams. The speed and spin on his pitches earned him the nickname "Cy" for "cyclone." He won 511 games, still the Major League record.

John Legend

Maya Lin

Jesse Owens

Who Ohioans Are

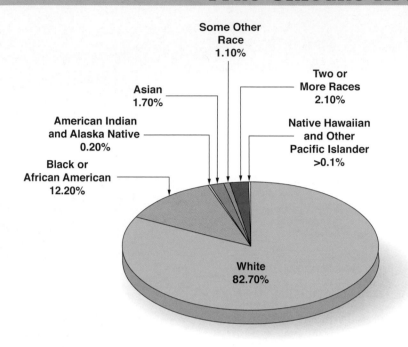

Some Other Race
1.10%

Two or More Races
2.10%

Asian
1.70%

American Indian and Alaska Native
0.20%

Native Hawaiian and Other Pacific Islander
>0.1%

Black or African American
12.20%

White
82.70%

Total Population
11,536,504

Hispanic or Latino (of any race):
• 354,674 people (3.1%)

Note: The pie chart shows the racial breakdown of the state's population based on the categories used by the US Bureau of the Census. The Census Bureau reports information for Hispanics or Latinos separately, since they may be of any race. Percentages in the pie chart may not add to 100 because of rounding.

Source: US Bureau of the Census, 2010 Census

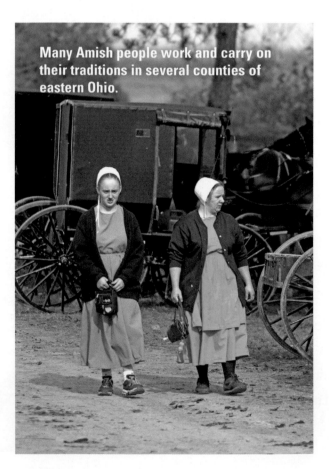

Many Amish people work and carry on their traditions in several counties of eastern Ohio.

The Amish Community

The Amish people originally immigrated to the United States from Switzerland during the eighteenth century. Their beliefs differed from other Christian religions in Europe. They came to America seeking religious freedom and a better life. Ohio's Holmes County, located between Columbus and Cleveland, is the home of the largest Amish community in the world. Today, nearly forty thousand Amish people live and work in these rolling hills in eastern Ohio.

Many Amish people do not believe in using modern conveniences such as electricity and automobiles. They dress plainly, practice their traditional ways of life, and live mostly off of the land. The

Ohio: The Astronaut Factory

Ohio has been the home state of twenty-five astronauts, including Neil Armstrong, the first man on the moon. Over twenty-two thousand hours have been logged in space by Ohio astronauts over the course of seventy-eight space flights. Cleveland has given us the most astronauts—seven people from the city have been to space.

Amish community welcomes visitors, and many people travel to these areas to experience the Amish way of life. The Amish have become known for their high-quality crafts, art, and furniture. In addition to shopping for these items, visitors come to Amish country to enjoy homemade food, visit museums, and take tours of Amish historical sites.

African Americans

In 1800, only 337 African Americans lived in Ohio, mostly in the southern part of the state. By 1860, a year before the start of the Civil War, more than 36,700 African Americans made Ohio their home. Despite the fact that Ohio was a Free State, African Americans still faced discrimination. Laws that denied them the right to vote were passed. In parts of southern Ohio, some white people broke the law by owning slaves. To avoid getting caught by authorities, farmers took their slaves to Kentucky to hide them when necessary.

After the Civil War, many African Americans moved to Ohio's cities to find work. Life in the city was not easy for black workers, and jobs that paid well were hard to find. Many African Americans worked in factories during this time, or as day laborers, nannies, housekeepers, or in restaurants. Out of fear of violence and racism, most black Ohioans lived in their own communities. Ohio lawmakers passed legislation during the nineteenth century that discriminated against African Americans' rights. Black people could not vote, serve on juries, or send their children to public school. Though most of these laws were reversed or overturned by the twentieth century, many black Ohioans continued to face racism. In the early twentieth century, Ohio's African-American population continued to climb as more people moved from the Southern United States to the North in search of work or a better life for their families. In 1959, the state passed the Ohio Civil Rights Act to help eliminate discrimination against African Americans in employment opportunities and access to businesses like restaurants and hotels.

Today's black Ohioans have prospered and succeeded in various fields. Some notable African Americans from Ohio include Pulitzer Prize winner Rita Dove, who in 1993 became the first African American—and the youngest person—to be named poet laureate of the United States. Also in 1993, Ohioan Toni Morrison became the first African American to receive the Nobel Prize in Literature.

Today, more than 1.4 million African Americans live in the state, making up the largest minority group in Ohio. They represent almost 12 percent of Ohio's population.

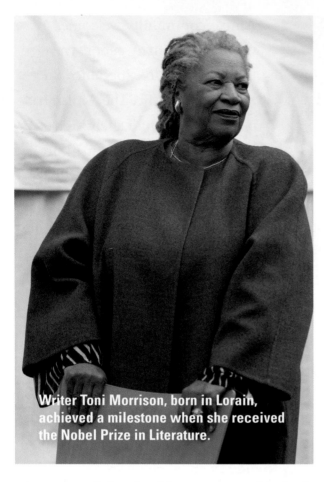

Writer Toni Morrison, born in Lorain, achieved a milestone when she received the Nobel Prize in Literature.

Other Cultures

Hispanic Americans and Asian Americans make up the next largest minorities in Ohio. Few Hispanics lived in Ohio until the 1960s. At that time, Latinos began immigrating to the United States in sizable numbers from Central and South American countries, Mexico, and the Caribbean in search of jobs. According to the 2010 US census, more than 350,000 Hispanics live in Ohio, accounting for about 3.1 percent of the state's population.

According to the 2014 census estimates, Asians are the fastest growing racial group in Ohio. The percentage of people of Asian descent living in Ohio climbed from 1.7 in 2010 to an estimated 2.0 percent in 2014. They trace their ancestries to China, Japan, India, Korea, the Philippines, Vietnam, and other Asian countries. State officials believe the rapid growth is due to Ohio companies doing increased business with Asian companies and the availability of medical and technology jobs. These jobs generally pay well and require high levels of education, making them appealing to many new immigrants who have experience in those fields. The presence of many colleges and universities in Ohio is a draw for many international students who come to the United States to study.

Education

Education has always been important to Ohioans. Early settlers built one-room schoolhouses made of logs. Before the first public schools in Ohio were established in 1825, parents paid for their children to attend school, sometimes in the form of

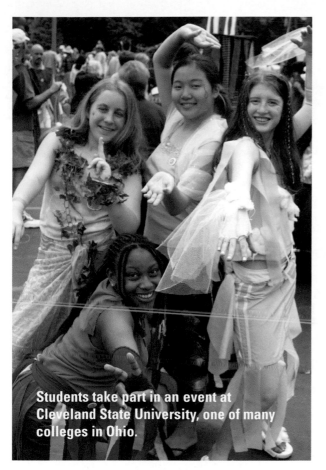

Students take part in an event at Cleveland State University, one of many colleges in Ohio.

goods to the teacher. In 1853, the state's first public high schools opened their doors.

Founded in 1833, Ohio's Oberlin College was the first US college to admit women. It was also one of the country's first colleges to admit African Americans. The college also played a role in abolitionist efforts before and during the Civil War. It was a key stop on the Underground Railroad. In 1858, a group of residents from Oberlin and a nearby town called Wellington rescued a fugitive slave named John Price and took him to Canada. The rescuers were jailed but later released, and the case, called the Oberlin-Wellington Rescue, was covered in newspapers across the country. Some historians consider this case to have played an important role in the start of the Civil War.

Today, Ohio is home to many well-respected colleges and universities. In 1862, the US Congress passed, and President Lincoln signed, the Morrill Act. This law allowed states to sell large areas of land donated to the states by the federal government in order to raise money to build public colleges. Thanks to this act, the college that is now the Ohio State University, also called Ohio State, was established in Columbus in 1870. Its first class had just twenty-four students. With nearly sixty thousand students today, Ohio State has grown into one of the country's largest universities. Other public and private colleges and universities include Ohio University (the state's first public college), Miami University, Oberlin College, Case Western Reserve University, Denison University, Baldwin Wallace University, Bowling Green State University, and Ohio Wesleyan University.

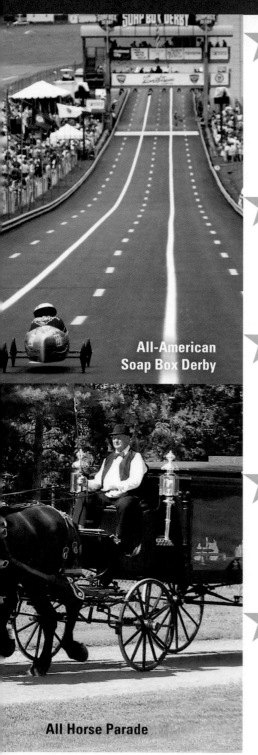

All-American Soap Box Derby

All Horse Parade

1. All-American Soap Box Derby

Each July, Akron hosts the All-American Soap Box Derby, a racing program in which kids ages seven to twenty drive homemade, engineless cars down an incline. The "Greatest Amateur Racing Event in the World" attracts racers from everywhere.

2. All Horse Parade

This September parade in Delaware kicks off the Delaware County Fair. Hundreds of horses are part of the parade, as well as vintage horse-drawn wagons, sleighs, and fire engines. Marching bands join the parade as well.

3. Americana Festival

Over seventy thousand people celebrate Independence Day in Centerville at the Americana Festival. A street fair, 5K race, and an arts and crafts exhibit are part of the fun, as well as many children's activities, including pony rides and a petting zoo.

4. Fabulous 50s Fling and Car Show

This June festival in Sugarcreek provides a chance to view classic automobiles, custom cars, and hot rods. The weekend includes car competitions, a 5K race, live music, and homemade food for sale. The festival has been held since 1991.

5. Festival Latino

Each August, Columbus residents celebrate the heritage of their Latin American community at the largest festival of its kind in Ohio. Traditional music is featured, as well as dance lessons, food, and arts and crafts.

6. Gourmet Food Truck Competition and Rally

The Gourmet Food Truck Competition and Rally brings dozens of food trucks to the Miami County Fairgrounds in Troy each May. Approximately ten thousand people attend the competition to sample food and raise funds for the fair.

7. Johnny Appleseed Festival

In late September, Lisbon hosts this festival to celebrate a beloved fall fruit: the apple. Attendees can enjoy all kinds of homemade products, including apple butter, apple fritters, apple dumplings, and apple pie. Activities include a parade, music, and more.

8. Ohio State Fair

More than eight hundred thousand people attend the annual Ohio State Fair, held in Columbus in early August. For more than 150 years, the fair has celebrated Ohio's products, people, and history.

9. Vectren Dayton Air Show

The Dayton Air Show is considered one of the country's top aviation events. The show, held each July, takes place at Dayton International Airport. Visitors can climb aboard some of the historic featured aircraft.

10. Window Wonderland

Window Wonderland is a holiday festival held in Wooster each November. Storefront windows are decorated with old-fashioned charm and holiday art. Attendees can enjoy a Christmas tree lighting and free hot cocoa and cookies.

Ohio State Fair

Vectren Dayton Air Show

The building with the green cupola is a replica
of the original state capitol in Chillicothe.

How the Government Works

O hio's constitution was created in 1802, one year before Ohio was admitted to the Union. The constitution affirms that the state government should be divided into three separate branches. The executive branch administers state laws, the legislative branch makes laws, and the judicial branch enforces and interprets laws. The state government is centered in the state capital, Columbus. This was not always the case, though. When Ohio first became a state in 1803, the capital was Chillicothe. It was later moved to Zanesville. Community leaders and politicians in Ohio continued to fight about where the capital should be. Finally, they decided to compromise and move the capital to the middle of the state, so Columbus was chosen.

Each of Ohio's eighty-eight counties, as well as each village and city, has a local government. An elected board of commissioners governs most counties. Many of Ohio's cities elect a mayor who enforces local laws passed by a council and manages the city government's budget. If a **municipality** has five thousand or more people in it according to the most recent US census, it is considered a city. If it has less than that, it is considered a village.

Various taxes help fund state and local governments. Residents often have to pay property, income, and sales taxes. Property taxes are based on the value of a person's home

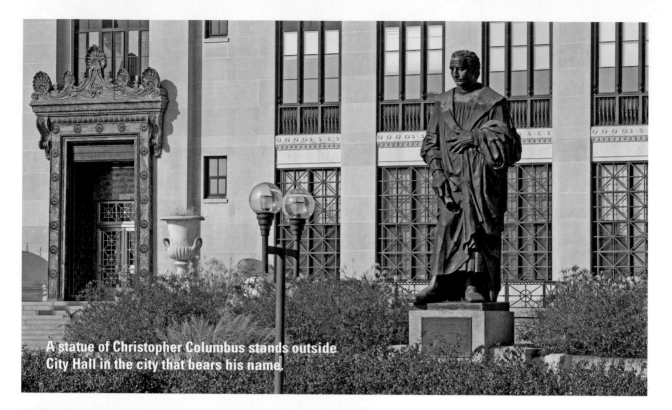
A statue of Christopher Columbus stands outside City Hall in the city that bears his name.

Cleveland Boosters

In the early 1980s, Cleveland mayor George Voinovich led a campaign to improve Cleveland's public image. The campaign's slogan was "New York's the Big Apple, but Cleveland's a plum." Voinovich even used a plum to throw out the first pitch at a game between the New York Yankees and the Cleveland Indians.

or other personal possessions, such as an automobile. When people buy certain products at a store, they pay a sales tax that might go partly to the state government and partly to the local government. State and other income taxes are taken out of a worker's paycheck or paid directly by people who are self-employed. State and local taxes help pay for schools, police and fire departments, town and state buildings, public libraries, and all kinds of government services, such as snow removal in the winter and lifeguards at public pools in the summer.

Ohio is often called the Mother of US Presidents. Seven presidents were born in Ohio: Ulysses S. Grant (eighteenth), Rutherford B. Hayes (nineteenth), James Garfield (twentieth), Benjamin Harrison (twenty-third), William McKinley (twenty-fifth), William Howard Taft (twenty-seventh), and Warren G. Harding (twenty-ninth). William Henry Harrison (ninth) was born in Virginia but lived in Ohio when he ran for president.

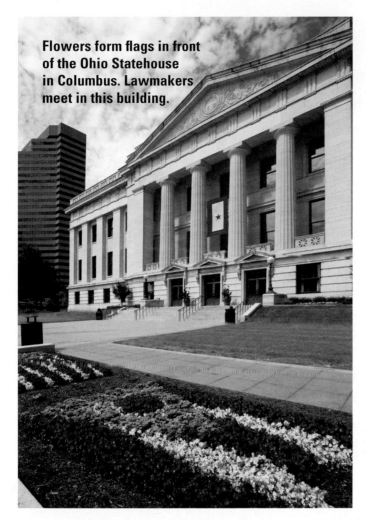
Flowers form flags in front of the Ohio Statehouse in Columbus. Lawmakers meet in this building.

Ohio is considered an influential state during presidential elections. This is also sometimes referred to as being a "swing state" or "battleground state." Usually, the candidate that wins in Ohio also wins the general election. In fact, no Republican has ever won the presidency without winning Ohio's electoral votes. The population is close to evenly split between Democrats and Republicans, and the state's electoral votes have been important to the overall election results many times before. Based on its population, Ohio has eighteen electoral votes.

Branches of Government

Executive

The governor is the head of the executive branch. The governor is responsible for managing a legislature-approved state budget, signing bills that are passed in the legislature, and appointing the directors of state departments and agencies. The governor is elected to a four-year term. He or she can serve only two terms in a row.

Legislative

Ohio's legislature is called the Ohio General Assembly. It has two houses, or chambers: the house of representatives and the senate. When the first meeting of the general assembly was held in Chillicothe on March 1, 1803, there were only thirty representatives in the house and fourteen members in the senate. In 1967, voters approved an amendment to the state constitution to increase those numbers. Now, Ohio has ninety-nine members in the house and thirty-three members in the senate. State senators may serve no more than two four-year terms. State representatives may serve no more than four two-year terms. The main role of these legislators is to debate and vote on proposed laws (bills). If the general assembly votes in favor of a bill, the governor may sign it into law.

Judicial

This branch is made up of the Ohio Supreme Court and many lower courts, including courts of appeals, courts of common pleas, county courts, municipal courts, and the court of claims. The main job of the state supreme court justices is to rule on cases in which a lower court's decision has been appealed by the losing party. State supreme court justices can decide whether or not a state law agrees with the state constitution. They also review all death penalty cases. One chief justice and six justices sit on the supreme court. They can be elected to an unlimited number of six-year terms.

Representation in Washington, DC

John Glenn was the first American to orbit the Earth, and he represented Ohio in the US Senate for twenty-five years.

Like all Americans, the people of Ohio are represented in the US Congress in Washington, DC. Each state elects two US senators, who serve six-year terms. There is no limit on the number of terms a US senator can serve. A state's population determines the number of people that it sends to the US House of Representatives. After the 2010 census, Ohio was entitled to sixteen representatives in the House. They can be elected to an unlimited number of two-year terms.

Ohio has had many standout representatives in the federal government, but John Glenn Jr. is one of the most unique. Glenn was born on July 18, 1921, in Cambridge, Ohio. In 1962, he became the first American astronaut to orbit Earth. After retiring as an astronaut, he represented Ohio as a US senator from 1974 to 1999. In 1998, at age seventy-seven, he returned to space, becoming the oldest person to travel outside Earth's atmosphere.

How a Bill Becomes a Law

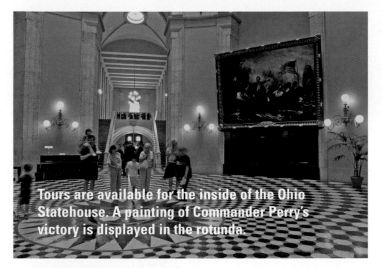

Tours are available for the inside of the Ohio Statehouse. A painting of Commander Perry's victory is displayed in the rotunda.

Members of the Ohio house and senate may either create new laws or change old ones. A law begins as a bill proposed by a state representative or a state senator, but the idea for a bill may come from an Ohio citizen. Any state resident with an idea for a new law can present it to his or her legislator.

In the legislature, a representative's or senator's proposal is written in legal language, recorded, and then considered. A bill introduced by a representative is first considered in the house, and a bill introduced by a senator is first considered in the senate.

First, the bill is debated by a committee of legislators. The committee might hold hearings to find out what members of the public and groups interested in the subject of the bill think about it. If the committee approves the bill, it is next debated in the full house or senate. If the members of that chamber pass the bill by a majority vote, it goes to the other chamber, where the process of considering and voting on the bill is repeated.

In Their Own Words

"If Ohio is not a member of the Union and we have some illegal members of the Senate and the House here, I should like to know it."
—Representative John Lyle of Texas, jokingly, on the day Ohio's constitution was officially ratified in 1953

If the second chamber passes the bill but makes changes to it first, then usually a committee made up of three members from each chamber works to come up with a final version of the bill. This final version must be passed again by both the house and the senate.

Once both chambers have approved a bill in exactly the same form, it is sent to the governor for his or her signature. If the governor signs the bill (or takes no action on it for ten days), it becomes a law. However, the governor may also veto, or reject, the bill if he or she does not agree with it. In that case, either the bill dies, or it may still become a law if both houses of the legislature again vote in favor of it—but this time by at least a three-fifths majority.

Nickie Antonio: Ohio House of Representatives, 2011-

A native of Lakewood, Antonio represents the thirteenth district in the Ohio House of Representatives, an area located in Cuyahoga County. She is a former member of the Lakewood City Council, a role she served in from 2005 to 2010. She is a graduate of Cleveland State University.

Ulysses S. Grant: US President, 1869-1877

Born in Point Pleasant in 1822, Ulysses S. Grant served as the eighteenth president of the United States. During the Civil War, Grant was one of the most successful Union generals, and he rose to become commander of all Union forces. He is buried in New York City, in the largest tomb in North America.

John Kasich: Governor, 2011-

Kasich has been a resident of Ohio since he attended college at Ohio State University. In addition to serving as governor, he also represented Ohio's twelfth district in the US House of Representatives and, before that, in Ohio's state senate. He ran for the Republican nomination in the 2016 presidential election.

OHIO ★ ★ ★ ★ ★

YOU CAN MAKE A DIFFERENCE

Contacting Lawmakers

Ohioans can take an active role in government and contact their representative and senator about issues of concern. Legislators are there to serve Ohioans and the state. To contact Ohio state legislators, go to:

www.legislature.state.oh.us

Enter your zip code or district number to find your senator or representative.

Your representatives in the US Congress are advocating for you on national matters. To contact your representative in Congress, go to:

www.house.gov/representatives/find

Enter your zip code to find contact information for your representative in Congress.

Cell Phone Use in Cars Restricted

Using a cell phone while driving a car is a dangerous habit, and one that leads to many accidents and injuries every year. Several states have passed laws banning texting while driving. Ohio became one of the latest to pass such a law in 2012, and citizens and advocacy groups played a role in helping the bill get passed.

The origins of the law can be traced back to 1999, when the city of Brooklyn, Ohio, banned cell phone usage behind the wheel. Since then, concerned citizens, law enforcement officials, and groups that promote safe driving have communicated with their representatives to ask for greater and more widespread regulation of texting while driving. In 2012, these efforts paid off when the Ohio House of Representatives passed House Bill 99, the law that banned hand-held cell phone usage while driving (hands-free devices may be used by adults). Governor John Kasich signed the bill in June 2012, and in August of that year, the statewide ban went into effect. The law also had additional specific regulations related to using a cell phone while driving. For people under age eighteen, using a cell phone in any way while driving is prohibited. For all Ohio residents, writing, reading, or sending texts, e-mails or any text-based communication is against the law.

Apples have been an important crop in Ohio since
Johnny Appleseed, whose real name was John Chapman,
planted his first orchards in the early nineteenth century.

Making a Living

The two main industries in Ohio's economic history are agriculture and manufacturing. Since the first permanent settlers in the Ohio region planted and cultivated seeds, agriculture has helped Ohioans make a living. Today, Ohio's farm products are used throughout the state, as well as exported to other states and countries.

Agriculture

Agriculture in Ohio has gone through good and bad times since statehood. The Great Depression hit Ohio farmers at the same time as a very long drought that caused crops to die. World War II, on the other hand, increased the demand for food, which benefited Ohio farmers. In the second half of the twentieth century, however, the number of farms in Ohio declined. The cost of food fell while the cost of living increased. Farmers were getting less for their crops at the same time that they were paying more for clothing, electricity, and machinery. In time, many people sold their farms and moved to the cities.

Ohio still has about eighty thousand farms, which cover about half the state. The major crops include soybeans, corn, hay, oats, and wheat. Most of these grains are fed to cattle, another important agricultural product. Ohio's cattle provide milk and beef. Ohio also is a major producer of hogs, ranks very high in the production of eggs, and makes more Swiss cheese than any other state.

Johnny Appleseed helped feed many of Ohio's first settlers with apples from his orchards.

Corn—one of Ohio's largest crops—is grown throughout the state. It is Ohio's second-most-valuable crop, after soybeans. Ohio ranks among the top ten corn-producing states in the country. Most of this corn is not eaten by people, though. More than half goes to feeding livestock, such as cows. Corn is also used to make a variety of products, from plastic and ethanol (a type of fuel) to cereal, cooking oil, glue, and ink.

Apples are another important state product. Ohioans are very proud of their famous apple farmer, John Chapman (1774–1845), known as Johnny Appleseed. Legend says that when Ohio became a state, Johnny Appleseed was traveling all over the region, planting apple orchards. Some of those trees, now two hundred years old, continue to bear fruit. The Johnny Appleseed Educational Center and Museum on the campus of Urbana University in Urbana honors the legendary frontiersman. Outside the museum are apple trees that started as cuttings from trees planted by Johnny Appleseed.

Ohio farmers also produce grapes and strawberries. Vegetables such as cucumbers and tomatoes are major crops in Ohio as well. Ohio farmers rank tenth in the United States for growing strawberries. More than 710 acres (287 hectares) of farmland are devoted just to strawberries. About 3 million pounds (1.4 million kilograms) of strawberries were produced in 2009. Strawberries are sometimes hard to grow, but Ohio's university researchers are working to find new types of strawberries to boost the state's production of this tasty fruit.

Manufacturing

Like agriculture, manufacturing has played a major role in the state economy. Ohio is a leading manufacturer of cars, trucks, motor vehicle parts, jet engines, airplane parts, and other transportation equipment. Some Ohioans work in factories that produce steel and tools. Ohio is one of the top steel-producing states in the country.

Ohio has many different kinds of factories. The city of Napoleon, for example, is home to the world's largest soup factory. Wellston claims to be the world's leading producer of frozen pizzas. Cincinnati has the biggest soap factory in the United States. Other major products made in Ohio include computer parts, rubber, electrical equipment, clay, glass, and paper and plastic items. Toledo is known as "the Glass City" because of its long history in innovation and manufacturing of glass products. Windows, bottles, windshields, and even glass art have been produced in Toledo. Several large glass companies were founded there, including Owens Corning, Libbey Glass, Pilkington North America, and Therma-Tru.

Many food-processing plants in Ohio handle the products that are grown on Ohio's farms. Some types of food-processing plants include those that pack meat, preserve and can fruits, and make dairy products.

Some Ohio manufacturers build high-tech products. Many **biotechnology** companies, which focus on using items found in nature to make products that improve lives, are launching or growing in northeast Ohio. These products could help cure diseases, create new energy sources, or support scientific research.

Mining

Mining also contributes to the state's economy. Ohio is one of the country's top coal-mining states. Coal is the state's most valuable mineral. For a long time, coal mining was unregulated by the state, and many coal miners worked in dangerous conditions.

Coal mining continues to be an important industry in Ohio. All of the coal is mined in eighteen counties in the eastern part of the state.

Automobiles

Biosciences

1. Advanced Energy

Advanced energy is a growing source of jobs in Ohio. These companies make new, more efficient ways of creating or harnessing the energy we use in our everyday lives—for example, fuel cells that power electric cars.

2. Aerospace and Aviation

Ohio is called the birthplace of aviation because it is the birthplace of Orville and Wilbur Wright, the inventors of the powered airplane. Today, the state is where new flight-related technology is researched, developed, and manufactured.

3. Automobiles

Automobile manufacturing is a $19.3 billion annual industry in the state. That is about 13 percent of total US output. Ohio is the second-largest producer of motor vehicles in the United States, after Michigan.

4. Banking

The financial services industry is one of Ohio's most important sectors. This industry includes commercial banks, financial advisor firms, credit card companies, and mortgage companies. The northeast region of the state is home to most of these jobs.

5. Biosciences

Bioscience, also known as life science, deals with living organisms or naturally-found matter to improve the lives of humans. The state's many universities and research facilities make Ohio an ideal location for more than two thousand bioscience firms.

6. Coal

Coal is Ohio's most important mined resource. The coal is mined in the eastern part of the state. Although miners have been digging for a long time, scientists believe more than 20 billion tons (18 billion metric tons) of coal remain.

7. Electronics

Instruments, controls, and electronics are an important part of the Ohio economy. In 2014, Ohio ranked fourth in the nation in employment in electrical equipment manufacturing. Many other companies in Ohio use these electronics, like car manufacturers.

8. Food Processing

A large number of skilled workers, access to materials suppliers, and plenty of fresh water from Lake Erie have helped Ohio's food processing industry thrive. The state is also home to many food-related research centers that help support these companies.

9. Salt

Ohio is home to large deposits of salt about 2,000 feet (600 m) underground. Ohio is one of the country's largest producers of rock salt, which is used to melt snow. The state mines about 4 million tons (3.6 million t) each year.

10. Soybeans

Although most of the state's soybeans are fed to cattle, some are used to make a nondairy substitute for milk. Soybeans are used in nonfood items such as hand cleaners, chemical cleaners, and lubricants that help machines run smoothly.

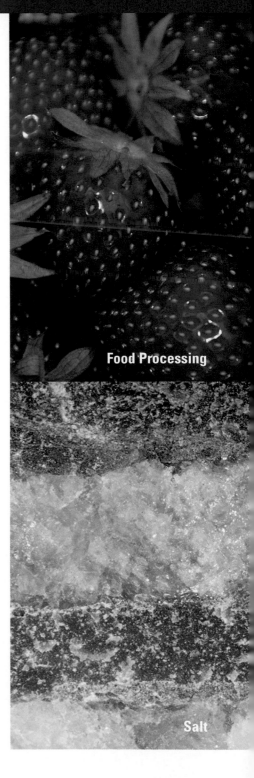

Food Processing

Salt

Recipe for Apple Chips

Apples are one of Ohio's tastiest and most nutritious crops. Choose your favorite kind of apple to make these apple chips. They're a healthy way to enjoy a sweet snack.

What You Need

2 cups (0.47 liters) unsweetened apple juice

1 cinnamon stick

2 whole apples

What To Do

- Ask an adult for help with the oven and stove. Heat oven to 250°F (120°C).

- Place the cinnamon stick and apple juice in a pot on the stove and bring to a low boil.

- Slice about 0.5 inches (1.3 cm) off the top and bottom of both apples. Use an apple corer or knife to remove the core.

- Slice each apple into very thin pieces crosswise (so you end up with circular pieces).

- Put the apple pieces into the boiling juice for four to five minutes.

- Remove the apples from the juice and pat dry with paper towels.

- Lay the chips on a baking sheet in a single layer. Make sure none of the pieces are touching.

- Bake 30 to 40 minutes. Apples should be brown and almost dry when finished.

- Turn off the oven. Let chips cool completely before removing from oven.

Plastic Pioneers

The five-county area around Akron has long been known as "Polymer Valley" because of the region's success in the research, development, and production of plastic. However, polymer companies are scattered throughout the state, and recently a concentration of these manufacturers has sprung up in southeastern Ohio as well.

The mines were harmful to the surrounding soil and environment. In 1947, Ohio passed the Strip Coal Mining Act. This helped make coal mining safer and lessen the impact on the environment of the lands surrounding mines.

Oil, natural gas, salt, clay, sandstone, and other minerals are also mined in Ohio. Sandstone and other minerals are used to construct buildings and highways. Many of these materials are also important to other Ohio industries, such as steel and glass manufacturing. Though mining is not as important to Ohio's economy as it was in the past, it is still a significant source of income. In 2014, the economic value of Ohio's coal and industrial minerals industry was valued at $2.18 billion.

The Business of Service

Most workers in Ohio have jobs in the service industry. This industry includes banking, health care, education, restaurants, retail stores, and hotels.

Tourism is a major part of the state's service industry as well. Each year, millions of people visit Ohio. Tourists relax on Ohio's lakeshore, hike through its parks, or visit the state's many historic sites and museums. Others enjoy the different festivals, fairs, and other events in Ohio's cities and towns. All these people spend money in the state. That money provides a profit for many service businesses and, when tourists make purchases, sales tax revenue for the state government and local governments. The tourism industry also employs many Ohioans, including tour guides, museum curators, hotel clerks, waitstaff, and store clerks.

Tourist Attractions

Tourists visiting Ohio have plenty to keep them busy. The state is home to many exciting historical, cultural, and recreational attractions. Tourists flock to Cedar Point amusement park in Sandusky in northern Ohio. Officially called "The Roller Coaster Capital of the World," Cedar Point holds the world record for the most roller coasters in one park— seventeen in all. Home to seventy-two rides as of 2015, Cedar Point now boasts more rides than any other amusement park in the world.

Cedar Point, which opened in Sandusky in 1870, has more roller coasters than any other amusement park in the world.

Medical Leader

Ohio's Cleveland Clinic is known around the world for its high success rates in treating many kinds of diseases, especially heart problems. Its main campus consists of forty-one buildings, and it operates fourteen other health centers in the Cleveland community. Cleveland Clinic also has facilities in Florida, Nevada, Canada, and Abu Dhabi, UAE.

Zoos are another state attraction. The Cincinnati Zoo and Botanical Garden is the second-oldest zoo in the United States. Animal lovers can also visit zoos in Columbus, Toledo, and Cleveland.

Ohio is home to several "halls of fame." The Rock and Roll Hall of Fame and Museum, located on Lake Erie in downtown Cleveland, opened in 1995. The museum's attention-grabbing glass pyramid attracts more than 7.5 million people each year. Visitors learn about the histories of their favorite rock stars and get an up-close look at music memorabilia. Sports fans and motorcycle enthusiasts can head to Canton's Pro Football Hall of Fame or the Motorcycle Hall of Fame Museum in Pickerington.

Historic Ohio draws tourists of all ages. The state pays homage to some of its flight pioneers with the Armstrong Air and Space Museum in Wapakoneta and the National Museum of the US Air Force in Dayton. The Air Force museum includes exhibits on the Wright brothers.

A high school softball team celebrates Cleveland's baseball history in front of a Bob Feller statue at Progressive Field.

Other famous Ohio natives have museums dedicated in their honor. Tourists can visit the Thomas Edison Birthplace Museum in Milan and learn about the inventor of the light bulb, the record player, and the motion picture camera. The life of one of history's greatest golfers is chronicled at the Jack Nicklaus Museum in his hometown of Columbus.

Science buffs can get their fill at the Goodyear World of Rubber in Akron or the Toledo Center of Science and Industry. Nature lovers can enjoy underground caves at Seneca Caverns in Bellevue or waterfalls and hiking at Wayne National Forest or Hocking Hills State Park in southeastern Ohio.

Professional sports provide enjoyment for Ohio residents and visitors alike. Ohio has teams in all four major professional sports leagues. Columbus has hockey's Blue Jackets. Cincinnati is home to baseball's Reds and football's Bengals. Cleveland has baseball's Indians, basketball's Cavaliers, and football's Browns. In addition, Columbus is home to the Crew of Major League Soccer. The team plays at Mapfre Stadium, the first soccer-specific stadium in the United States.

The Ohio State University competes in more than two dozen varsity sports and has one of the top-ranked football teams in the country. The Buckeyes play in the state's largest stadium.

The Future

Like residents of many other states, Ohioans are trying to protect their environment and, at the same time, encourage growth. More businesses might mean more jobs and money, but do they also mean more pollution and damage to the natural environment? Developing high-technology and other "clean" industries may help Ohioans to have comfortable lives and still preserve the beauty of their state.

OHIO
STATE MAP

LAKE ERIE

Conneaut
Ashtabula
Headlands Beach State Park
Euclid
90
20
6
Cleveland
322
Pymatuning Reservoir
Cedar Point National Wildlife Refuge
Ottawa National Wildlife Refuge
Crystal Cave Glacial Grooves State Memorial
Mosquito Creek Reservoir
5
Shenango River Lake
Great Lake Plains
Toledo
Sandusky Bay
Sandusky
Lorain
Elyria
Warren
7
80
90
475
Fallen Timbers Battlefield and Ft. Miamis National Historic Site
6
80
90
Defiance
Bowling Green
Fremont
Seneca Caverns
Norwalk
Cuyahoga Valley National Park
77
480
80
Kent
Meander Reservoir
Youngstown
Maumee River
Medina
Akron
76
Berlin Lake
80
76
24
Fort Defiance Memorial
127
Findlay
23
20
250
60
Wooster
Canton
30
Indian Trail Caverns
39
Till Plains
Lima
30
Mansfield
39
62
77
250
39
7
Indian Lake
Scioto River
Marion
71
60
22
Steubenville
68
Campbell Hill
Delaware
Grand Lake St. Marys
Ohio Caverns
Alum Creek State Park
Great Circle Earthworks
Newark
Cambridge
22
Appalachian Plateau
127
75
Urbana
Columbus
Zanesville
Senecaville Lake
Greenville
Springfield
270
70
Blue Rock State Forest
Muskingum River
60
70
Dayton
Buckeye Lake
127
35
Washington Court House
23
Lancaster
Marietta
Caesar Creek Lake
22
Circleville
Oxford
Middletown
Hopewell Culture National Historical Park
Athens
50
Hamilton
Chillicothe
35
Leo Petroglyph State Memorial
7
74
50
62
Rocky Fork Lake
50
275
Serpent Mound State Memorial
68
Wayne National Forest
Cincinnati
52
Portsmouth
52
Ohio River

miles
0   30

N
W   E
S

	Interstate Highway		City or Town		Highest Point in the State
	U.S. Highway		National Forest		State Forest
	State Highway		Historic Site		State Park
	State Capital		Wildlife Refuge		National Park

74   Ohio

OHIO ★ ★ ★ ★ ★
MAP SKILLS

1. The city of Newark is located near which interstate highway?

2. Which city is located at the most northeastern point of the state?

3. If you were in Urbana and traveled south on US Highway 68, what city would you reach first?

4. What direction should you travel from Chillicothe in order to reach Wayne National Forest?

5. Which state park is located closest to Ohio's capital city?

6. What is the name of the river closest to Cincinnati?

7. If you traveled east on US Highway 6 from Bowling Green, which city would you reach first?

8. Which lake is located southwest of Newark?

9. How many cities are located on or very near to US Highway 23 in Ohio?

10. Which body of water is located east of Middletown?

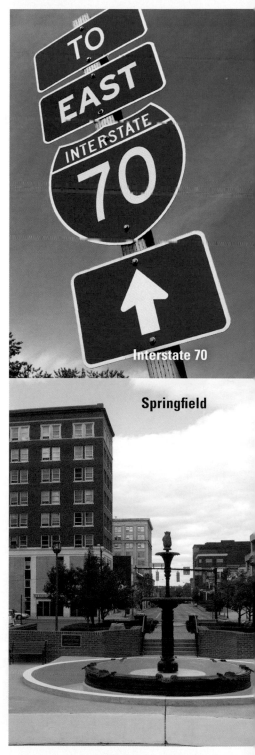

Interstate 70

Springfield

10. Caesar Creek Lake
9. Six: Marion, Delaware, Columbus, Circleville, Chillicothe, and Portsmouth.
8. Buckeye Lake
7. Fremont
6. Ohio River
5. Alum Creek State Park
4. Southeast
3. Springfield
2. Conneaut
1. Interstate 70.

State Flag, Seal, and Song

Ohio's flag is shaped like a pennant with red and white stripes and a large blue triangle. The triangle has seventeen white stars in it. The thirteen stars grouped around the circle represent the thirteen original colonies. The other four white stars near the corner of the triangle symbolize Ohio becoming the seventeenth state. The white "O" stands for "Ohio," and the red center symbolizes the buckeye. The blue triangle represents the state's hills and valleys. The red and white stripes stand for Ohio's roads and waterways.

The Ohio state seal depicts a rising sun with thirteen rays, representing the original colonies. The sun is rising over Mount Logan. In the middle ground is the Scioto River. There is also a bundle of wheat, which stands for Ohio's agriculture and bounty. Next to the wheat is a bundle of seventeen arrows, which refer to Ohio's being the seventeenth state to join the Union.

A song called "Beautiful Ohio" became the state's official song in 1969. The lyrics were written by Ballard McDonald and the music by Mary Earl. View the song's lyrics at: **www.50states.com/songs/ohio.**

Glossary

beach ridges   Sandy deposits that rise above the otherwise flat ground.

biotechnology   The science of using living or naturally occurring things to create new products that improve lives.

breechcloth   A traditional Native American cloth garment worn around the hips, usually by men.

decimated   When a large part of a population, either human, animal, or plant, is killed or destroyed. This can also refer to cities or areas.

endangered   When an animal or plant species is harmed or destroyed and in danger of extinction.

famine   A wide-reaching food shortage. The Irish potato famine caused mass starvation and brought many Irish immigrants to Ohio during the 1840s.

flint   A very hard, fine-grained mineral that has sharp edges and throws off a spark when struck with steel.

Great Depression   A time of declining economic activity in the worldwide economy from the late 1920s through the 1930s.

hierarchy   The way a group of people is organized into ranks.

horticulture   The science of growing plants, including fruits, vegetables, and decorative varieties such as flowers.

induct   To admit as a member or ceremonially install in a position or office.

municipality   A city, town, district, or other area with its own government.

outpost   A fort or military camp located a great distance from the main force or headquarters.

ratified   Confirmed by agreeing to or giving approval.

US Census Bureau   A government agency responsible for gathering and producing data about the American people.

More About Ohio

BOOKS

Jerome, Kate Boehm. *Ohio: What's So Great About This State?* Mount Pleasant, SC: Arcadia Publishing, 2010.

Kurtz, Jane. *Celebrating Ohio.* 50 States to Celebrate. Boston: Houghton Mifflin Harcourt, 2015.

Marsh, Carole. *Ohio Native Americans.* Peachtree City, GA: Gallopade International, 2004.

Schonberg, Marcia. *Ohio History.* Portsmouth, NH: Heinemann, 2009.

WEBSITES

The Official State Website—Kids Page
ohio.gov/government/kids

The Ohio Digital Library—Kids Section
ohioebooks.org/kids

Ohio History Connection
www.ohiohistory.org

ABOUT THE AUTHORS

Joyce Hart is a native of Ohio who graduated from the University of Oregon and raised her children in Eugene. A freelance author and editor, she enjoys traveling the backroads of the Pacific Northwest.

Lisa M. Herrington is a children's writer and editor who has extensive family in the Cleveland and Youngstown areas. She enjoys visiting the shores of Lake Erie. She lives in Trumbull, Connecticut, with her husband and daughter.

Kerry Jones Waring is a writer and editor from Buffalo, New York, where she lives with her husband and son.

Index

Page numbers in **boldface** are illustrations. Entries in **boldface** are glossary terms.

Index